CW00767792

GREAT
ANSWERS
to
TOUGH
INTERVIEW
QUESTIONS

HOW TO GET THE JOB YOU WANT

Third Edition

Martin John Yate

KOGAN
PAGE

Acknowledgements

My thanks to the following people. From the employment services world: Dunhill Personnel System presidents – Brad Brin of Milwaukee, Warren Mahan of Maine, Leo Salzman of Columbus, Dave Bontempo of Southampton, Paul and Pat Erickson of Shawnee Mission, Jim Fowler of Huntsville (and Ray Johnson), Stan Hart of Troy, Mike Badgett of Cherry Hills Village, and John Webb and everyone in beautiful San Antonio.

Thanks also to Don Kipper of Ernst & Whinney, Dan O'Brien of Grumman Aerospace, Amy Margolis and Kathy Seich of Merrill Lynch, Roger Villanueva of IMS, Victor Lindquist of Northwestern University, Ed Fitzpatrick of the University of Michigan, and Mary Giannini of Columbia University.

And special thanks to Jill, for being the brightest star in my firmament.

First published in the United States of America
in 1985 by Bob Adams Inc, Boston, Massachusetts
Copyright © Martin John Yate 1985

Third edition 1992
Copyright © Peregrine McCoy Ltd 1992

First UK edition published in Great Britain
in 1986 by Kogan Page Ltd, 120 Pentonville Road, London N1 9JN
Second revised edition 1988, reprinted with revisions 1989, 1990, 1991
Third revised edition 1992
Reprinted 1992

British Library Cataloguing in Publication Data

A CIP record for this book is available
from the British Library.

Typeset by DP Photosetting, Aylesbury, Bucks
Printed in England by Clays Ltd, St Ives plc

Contents

Introduction

Why another book about interviewing? Because the others stop at that critical point when the tough questions start flying. They lack the practical advice of what to do in the heat of battle. *Great Answers to Tough Interview Questions* first helps you to arrange interviews, then gets right to the heart of your biggest interview dread: 'How on earth do I answer that one?' It takes command where the others admit defeat.

Here you get over one hundred and sixty of the tough, sneaky, mean and low-down questions that interviewers love to throw at you. I show you what the interviewer is seeking to find out about you with each one, and explain how best to reply. After each explanation you get a sample answer and a unique way to customise the sample to your individual circumstances. The examples themselves come from real life, something that someone like you did on the job that got them noticed and helped them to get ahead in their careers.

Perhaps you are trying to land your first job, or are returning to the workplace, or maybe you're a seasoned executive taking another step up the ladder of success. Whoever you are, this book will help you because every interviewer consistently tries to evaluate every candidate in the same three ways: Are you able to do the job? Are you willing to put in the effort to make the job a success? And finally, the interviewing manager wants to know if you are manageable. You will learn how to demonstrate your superiority in each of these areas, under all interview conditions.

In interviewing for a new job you will meet two types of interviewer. The first is the 'consciously competent', a professionally trained interviewer who has a carefully structured plan for revealing all your warts and blemishes. The second is the 'unconscious incompetent', who is equally dangerous and bases judgements on gut reactions and nothing more. The book helps you to identify and shine with both of these characters.

The job interview is a measured and ritualistic mating dance in which the best partners whirl away with the glittering prizes.

The steps of this dance are the thrust and parry, give-and-take, question-and-response that make meaningful business conversation. Learn the steps and you too can join the dance.

Your partner in the dance is the interviewer, who will lead with tough questions that carry subtleties hidden from the untrained ear. You will learn how to recognise these questions within questions. And with this knowledge you will be cool, calm and collected while other candidates are falling apart with attacks of interview nerves.

How do you discover hidden meanings in questions? I recently heard a story about a young woman who was doing very well at an interview for a high pressure job in a television studio. The interviewer wanted to know how she would react in the sudden stressful situations common in TV and got his answer by asking, 'You know, I don't really think you are suitable for the job. Wouldn't you be better off in another company?' The job hunter got up with wounded pride and stormed out in a huff. She never knew how close she was to success or how easy it would have been to land that job. The interviewer smiled; he'd caught her out with a tough question. Did the interviewer mean what he said? What was really behind the question? How could she have handled it and got the job? The great answers to tough questions like that and many others are awaiting you.

The job interview has many similarities to good social conversation. Job offers always go to the interviewee who can turn a one-sided examination of skills into a dynamic exchange between two professionals. Here you will learn the techniques to excite and hold your interviewer's attention, at the same time promoting yourself as the best candidate for the job.

Great Answers will carry you successfully into and out of the worst interviews you could ever face. It is written in four interconnected parts. Each readies you for the interview and selection process in a distinctive way. 'The Well-Stocked Briefcase' gets you ready for the fray. You will quickly learn to build a curriculum vitae with broad appeal, plus a unique customising technique guaranteed to make your application stand out as something special. You will also learn how to tap into the job openings at all levels that never reach the newspapers.

We are a nation anxious to work, yet the cry goes out that there is no work to be had. Some find it easier to cry out against the darkness than dare to light a candle lest a finger get burned. When you know where and how to look you will find the mysterious hidden job market the headhunters talk about –

thousands of jobs at all levels that never reach the newspapers. You will learn how to tap in at the source.

Once you are ready for action 'Getting to Square One' examines all the approaches to getting job interviews and teaches you simple and effective ways to set up multiple interviews. The section includes techniques to steer you successfully through those increasingly common telephone interviews.

'Great Answers to Tough Interview Questions' gives you just that, and teaches you some valuable business lessons that will contribute to your future success. All successful companies look for the same things in their employees, and everything they are looking for you have or can develop. Not possible? I'll prove it to you with the twenty key personality traits which every success-ful company wants you to show them.

'Finishing Touches' assures that 'out-of-sight-out-of-mind' will not apply to you after leaving the interview. You will even discover how to get a job offer after you have been turned down for the position, and how to negotiate the best salary and package for yourself when a job offer is made. Most important, the sum of these techniques will give you tremendous self-confidence when you go to an interview: no more jitters, no more sweaty palms.

If you want to know how business works and what know-how business people look for in employees, how to locate, approach and sell yourself at the interview, this book is for you.

Great Answers to Tough Interview Questions delivers what you need to win the job of your dreams. Now get to it – step ahead in your career when you give great answers to tough interview questions.

Part 1
The Well-Stocked Briefcase

Out there in the concrete 'forest' of your profession hide many companies. Some major corporations, some small family affairs, and some in between. They all have something in common, and that's *problems*. To solve these problems, companies need people. Anyone who is ever employed for any job is a problem-solver. Think about your present job function. What problems would occur if you weren't there? That's why you were hired – to take care of those problems.

Being a problem-solver is good, but companies prefer to appoint someone who also understands what business is all about. There are three lessons you should remember:

1. Companies are in business to make money. People have loyalty to companies; companies have loyalty only to the bottom line. They make money by being more economical and saving money. They make money by being efficient and saving time. And if they save time, they save money, and have more time to make more money.

2. Companies and you are exactly alike. You both want to make as much money as possible in as short a time as possible. This allows you to do the things you really want with the rest of your time.

3. When the economy is good, you have the whip hand and can dictate the terms. This is called a *seller's market*. When the economy is bad, the employer has the whip hand and can dictate the terms. This is called a *buyer's market*.

Lesson 1 tells you the three things every company is interested in. Lesson 2 recognises that you really have the same goals as the company. Lesson 3 says that anyone with any sense wants to be in a seller's market.

If you look for jobs one at a time, you put yourself in a buyer's market. If you implement my advice you will have multiple interviews because you'll be able to handle the toughest questions, and you'll get multiple job offers. This will give you the whip hand and will put you in a seller's market.

Operating in a seller's market requires knowing who, where and what your buyers are in the market for, then being ready with the properly packaged product.

In Part 1 you will see how to identify all the companies that could be in need of your services. You will discover names of the chairman, those on the board, those in management; company sales volume; complete lines of company services or products; and size of the operation. You will evaluate and package your professional skills in a method guaranteed to have appeal to every employer. And you will discover highly desirable professional skills that you never thought you had.

A well-stocked briefcase requires more than looking idly through the sits vacant. It means a little discipline, a little effort. But aren't your professional goals worth the effort? It will take a couple of days' work to get geared up.

Your first action should be a trip to the library (taking sufficient paper and pens). Take some sandwiches; there is no feeling in the world like eating lunch on the library steps.

Chapter 1

Discovering What's Out There

At the library, walk in purposefully and ask for the reference
section. When you find it, wander around for a few minutes
before staking a claim. You will discover that libraries are a good
place to watch the human race, so get the best seat in the house.
Make sure you have a clear view of the librarian's desk. When
you need a rest, that's where all the comic relief takes place.

Reference books

There are a number of reference books you can consult, and they
are listed in the Bibliography. I won't waste space teaching you
how to use them here – the librarian will be happy to do that.

Your goal is to identify and build personalised dossiers on the
companies in your chosen geographic area. Do not be judgemen-
tal about what and who they might appear to be: you are fishing
for possible job openings, so cast your net wide and list them all.

Take a pad of paper, and using a separate sheet for each
company, copy all the relevant company information on to that
piece of paper. So that we agree on 'relevant', take a look at the
example on the following page.

Here you see the names of the company's chairman and
managing director, a description of the complete lines of company services and/or products, the size of the company, and the
locations of its various branches. Of course, if you find other
interesting information, copy it down by all means. For instance,
you might come across information on growth or shrinkage in a
particular area of a company; or you might read about recent
acquisitions the company has made. Write it down.

All this information will help you to shine at the interview in
three different ways. Your knowledge creates a favourable
impression when first meeting the company; that you made an
effort is noticed. That no one else bothers is a second benefit. And
third, the combination says that you respect the company, and

Company Ltd
Head Office: 231 Piccadilly
                London W1V 9TY
Phone: 071-246 8091
Personnel (George Wanstead, dir) 071-246 8093

MD: Gordon Blair
Chairman: Sir Geoffrey Jones
Export Sales director: David Macdonald

Company produces high performance sports cars
at its Northampton plant, supplies tooling
and key components for local assembly
overseas. Exports expanding to markets in
W. Germany, US and Middle East.

Turnover (1990)   £4.5m
Profits + 11.5% from 1989

Recently acquired machine tool company
in Dusseldorf.

therefore, by inference, the interviewer; this helps to set you
apart from the herd.

All your effort has an obvious short-term value in helping you
to win job offers. It also has value in the long term, because you
are building a personalised reference work of your industry/

speciality/profession that will help you throughout your career whenever you wish to make a job change.

Unfortunately, no single reference work is complete. Their very size and scope means that most are just a little out of date at publication time. Also, no single reference work lists every company. Because you don't know what company has the very best job for you, you need to research as many businesses in your area as possible, and therefore you will have to look through additional reference books.

Be sure to check any specialised guides mentioned in the Bibliography, including the *Key British Enterprises* and your local manufacturing directory.

At the end of the day, pack up and head for home. Remember on the way to purchase a map of your area, drawing pins and small size stick-on labels for implementing the next stage of your plan.

Put your map on the wall. Attach a string to a drawing pin, stick the pin on the spot where you live, and draw concentric circles at intervals of one mile. In a short space of time, you will have defaced a perfectly good map, but you'll have a *physical* outline of your job-hunting efforts.

Next, take out the company biographies prepared at the library and write 'No 1' on the first. Find the firm's location on the map and mark it with a drawing pin. Finally, mark an adhesive label 'No 1' and attach it to the head of the pin. As you progress, a dramatic picture of your day's work appears. Each pin-filled circle is a territory that needs to be covered, and each of those pins represents a potential job.

It is likely you will be back at the library again, finishing off this reference work and preparing your curriculum vitae. The research might take a few days. Try walking to the library the next time. Not only is it cheaper (a sound reason in itself), but the exercise is very important to you. You are engaged in a battle of wits, and the healthier you are physically, the sharper you will be mentally. You need your wits about you, because there are always well-qualified people looking for the best jobs. Yet it is not the most qualified who always get the job. It is the person who is best prepared who wins every time. Job hunters who knock 'em for six at the interview are those who do the homework and preparation that a failure will not do. Do a little more walking. Do a little more research.

Newspapers

Almost everybody looking for a new job buys the newspaper and then carefully misuses it. One story tells of a job hunter who started by waiting for the Sunday paper to be published. He read the paper and circled six jobs. He phoned the first to find it had already been filled and, in the process, was snubbed by someone whose voice had yet to break, requesting that he write in the future and send a CV. As anything is better than facing telephone conversations like that, the job hunter didn't ring the other five companies, but took a week to write a CV that no one would read, let alone understand. He sent it to a dozen companies and waited a week for someone to phone. Waited another week. Kicked the cat. Felt bad about that, worse about himself, and had a couple of drinks. Phone rang, someone was interested in the CV but, unfortunately, not in someone who slurred his words at lunch-time. Felt worse, stayed in bed late. Phone rings: an interview! Felt good, went to the interview. They will contact in a few days. They don't, and in the calls to them, everybody is mysteriously unavailable. The job hunter begins to feel like a blot on the landscape. This is obviously an extreme example, but the story is a little too close to the bone for many, and it illustrates the wrong way to use the paper when you're looking for a job.

Unfortunately, people usually use either the newspaper *or* reference books, but rarely both. They run the risk of ending up in the buyer's market. Not a good place to be.

While reference books give you bags of hard information about a company, they tell you little about specific job openings. Newspapers, on the other hand, tell you about specific jobs that need filling now, but give you few hard facts about the company. The two types of research should complement each other. Often you will find ads in the newspaper for companies you have already researched. What a powerful combination of information this gives you going in the door to the interview!

The correct way to use newspapers is to identify all companies that are currently recruiting. Write down the pertinent details of each particular job opening on a separate piece of paper as you did earlier with the reference books. Include the company's name, address, phone number and contact names.

In addition to finding openings that bear your particular title, look for all the companies that need staff regularly in your field. The fact that your job is not being advertised does not mean a company is not looking for you; if a company is in a recruiting mode, a position for you might be available. In the instances when a company is active but has not been advertising specifically for your skills, write down all relevant company contact data. You could be the solution to a problem that has only just arisen, and should get in touch.

It is always a good idea to examine back issues of the newspapers. These can provide a rich source of job opportunities that remain unfilled from prior advertising efforts.

The 'hidden' jobs

The reason you *must* use a combination of reference books and advertisements is that companies tend to recruit in cycles. When you rely exclusively on newspapers, you miss those companies just about to start or just ending their cycles. This comprehensive research is the way to tap what the business press refers to as the 'hidden' job market. It is paramount that you have as broad a base as possible – people know people who have *your* special job to fill.

With the addition of all these companies to your map, you will have a glittering panorama of prospects, the beginnings of a dossier on each one, and an efficient way of finding any company's exact location. This is useful for finding your way to an interview and in evaluating the job offers coming your way.

Adequate research and preparation are the very foundation for performing well at interviews. And the more interviews you have, the more your research skills will increase; they are the first step to putting yourself in a seller's market.

Chapter 2
All Things to All People –
Packaging the Curriculum Vitae

Interviewers today are continually asking for detailed examples of your past performance. They safely assume you will do at least as well (or as poorly) on the new job as you did on the old one, and so the examples you give will seal your fate. Therefore, you need to examine your past performance in a practical manner that will ensure you handle these questions correctly.

This chapter will show you how to identify the examples from your past that will impress any interviewer. There is a special bonus; you will also get the correctly packaged information for an excellent curriculum vitae. Two birds with one stone.

CVs, of course, are important, and there are two facts you must know about them. First, you are going to need one. Second, no one will want to read it. The average interviewer has never been trained to interview effectively, probably finds the interview as uncomfortable as you do, and will do everything possible to avoid discomfort. CVs are therefore used more to screen people *out* than screen them *in*. So your CV must be all things to all people.

Another hurdle to leap is avoiding the specialisation of your skills in the CV. A cold hard fact is that the first person to see your CV is often in the personnel department. This office screens for many different jobs and cannot be expected to have an in-depth knowledge of every speciality within the company – or its jargon.

For these reasons, your CV must be easy to read and understand, short, use words that are familiar to the reader and that have universal appeal. Most important, it should portray you as a problem-solver.

While this chapter covers ways to build an effective CV, its main goal is to help you perform better at the interview. You will achieve this as you evaluate your professional skills according to the exercises. In fact, you are likely to discover skills and achievements you didn't even know you had. A few you will use in your CV (merely a preview of coming attractions); the others you will use to knock 'em for six at the interview.

How to draft your CV

A good starting point is your current or last job title. Write it down. Then jot down all the other different titles you have heard that describe this job. When you are finished, follow it with a three- or four-sentence description of your job functions. Don't think too hard about it, just do it. The titles and descriptions are not carved in stone. This written description is the beginning of the CV-building exercises. You'll be surprised at what you've written; it'll read better than you had thought.

All attributes that you discover and develop in the following exercises are valuable to an employer. You possess many desirable traits, and these exercises help to reveal and to package them.

EXERCISE 1

Re-read the written job description, then write down your most *important* duty or function. Follow this with a list of the skills or special training necessary to perform that duty. Next, list the achievements of which you are most proud in this area. It could look something like this:

Duty	Train and motivate sales staff of six.
Skills	Formal training skills. Knowledge of market and ability to make untrained sales staff productive. Ability to keep successful salespeople motivated and tied to the company.
Achievements	Reduced turnover 7 per cent; increased sales 14 per cent.

The potential employer is most interested in the achievements, those things that make you stand out from the crowd. Try to appeal to a company's interests by conservatively estimating what your achievements meant to your employer. If your achievements saved time, estimate how much. If you saved money, how much? If your achievements made money for the company, how much? Beware of exaggeration; if you were part of a team, identify your achievements as such. It will make your claims more believable and will demonstrate your ability to work with others.

23

Achievements, of course, differ according to your profession. Most of life's jobs fall into one of these broad categories:

- Sales
- Management and administration
- Technical and production.

While it is usual to cite the differences between these major job functions, it is far more valuable to you to recognise what they have in common. In sales, cash volume is important. In management or administration, the parallel is time saved, which is money saved; saving money is just the same as making money for your company. In the technical and production areas, increasing production (doing more in less time) accrues exactly the same benefits to the company. Job titles may differ, yet all employees have the same opportunity to benefit their employers and, in turn, themselves.

The economic recession in the late eighties/early nineties has irrevocably changed the workplace. Today, companies are doing more with less; they are leaner, have higher expectations of their employees, and plan to keep it that way. The people who get jobs and get ahead today are those with a basic understanding of business goals. And successful job candidates are those who have the best interests of the company and its profitability constantly in mind.

EXERCISE 2
This simple exercise helps you to get a clear picture of your achievements. If you were to talk to your supervisor to discuss a rise, what achievements would you want to discuss? List all you can think of, quickly. Then come back and flesh out the details.

EXERCISE 3
This exercise is particularly valuable if you feel you can't see the wood for the trees.

Problem   Think of a job-related problem you had to face in the last couple of years. Come on, everyone can remember a problem.

Solution   Describe your solution to this problem, step by step. List everything you did.

Results   Finally, consider the results of your solution, in terms that would have value to an employer: money earned or saved; time saved.

EXERCISE 4

Now, a valuable exercise that turns the absence of a negative into a positive. This one helps you to look at your job in a different light and accents important but often overlooked areas that help to make you special. Begin discovering for yourself some of the key personal traits that all companies look for.

First, consider actions that if not carried out properly would affect the goal of your job. If this is difficult, remember an incompetent co-worker. What did he or she do wrong? What did he or she do differently from *competent* employees?

Now, turn the absence of these negatives into positive attributes. For example, think of the employee who never managed to get to work on time. You could honestly say that someone who *did* come to work on time every day was punctual and reliable; believed in systems and procedures; was efficiency-minded and cost- and profit-conscious.

If you have witnessed the reprimands and ultimate termination of that persistently late employee, then you will see the value of the *positive* traits in the eyes of an employer. The absence of negative traits makes you a desirable employee, but no one will know unless you tell them. On completion of the exercise, you will be able to make points about your background in a positive fashion. You will set yourself apart from others, if only because others do not understand the benefits of projecting all their positive attributes.

EXERCISE 5

Potential employers and interviewers are always interested in people who:

- are efficiency-minded;
- have an eye for economy;
- follow procedures;
- are profit-oriented.

Proceed through your work history and identify the aspects of your background that exemplify these traits. These newly discovered personal pluses will not only be woven into your CV, but will be reflected in the nature of your answers when you get to the interview.

Packaging the data

You now need to take some of this knowledge and package it in a curriculum vitae. There are three standard types of CV:

1. *Chronological.* The most frequently used format. Use it when your work history is stable and your professional growth is consistent. Avoid it if you have experienced performance problems or have made frequent job changes.
2. *Functional.* Use this type if you have been unemployed for long periods of time or have jumped jobs too frequently. A functional CV is created without employment dates or company names, and concentrates on skills and responsibilities.
3. *Prioritised.* The prioritised CV can be useful if you have changed careers, or when current responsibilities don't relate specifically to the job you want. It is written with the most relevant experience to the job you're seeking placed first.

Notice that each style is designed to minimise certain undesirable traits. As few of us are perfect (present company excepted), most people find it most effective to write a combination CV.

Employers are wary of the 'too-perfect' CV. With this in mind, there are just seven rules for creating a workmanlike one.

1. Use the most general of job titles. You are, after all, a hunter of interviews, not of specific titles. Cast your net wide. Use a title that is specific enough to put you in the field, yet vague enough to elicit further questions. A job title can be made specifically vague by adding the term 'specialist' (eg Computer Specialist, Administration Specialist, Production Specialist).
2. Avoid giving a job objective. If you must state a specific job as your goal, couch it in terms of contributions you can make in that position. Do not state what you expect of the employer.
3. Do not state your current salary. If you are earning too little or too much, you could rule yourself out before getting your foot in the door. Do not mention your desired salary for the same reason.
4. Remember that people get great joy from pleasant surprises. Show a little gold now, but let the interviewer discover the motherlode at the interview.
5. Take whatever steps are necessary to keep the CV's length

to a two-page maximum. No one reads long CVs; they are boring, and every company is frightened that if it lets in a windbag, it will never get him or her out again.

6. Your CV must be typed. As a rule of thumb, three pages of double-spaced, handwritten notes make one page of typescript.

7. Finally, emphasise your achievements and problem-solving skills. Keep the CV general.

The Executive Briefing

A general curriculum vitae does have drawbacks. First, it is too general to relate your qualifications to each specific job. Second, more than one person will probably be interviewing you, and that is a major stumbling block. While you will ultimately report to one person, you may well be interviewed by other team members. When this happens, the problems begin.

A manager says, 'Spend a few minutes with this candidate and tell me what you think.' Your general CV may be impressive, but the manager rarely outlines the job being filled or the specific qualifications he or she is looking for adequately. This means that other interviewers do not have any way to qualify you fairly and specifically. While the manager will be looking for specific skills relating to projects at hand, personnel will be trying to match your skills to the job-description manual vagaries, and the other interviewers will flounder in the dark because no one told them what to look for. This naturally could reduce your chances of landing a job offer.

Professionals in the employment services industry face this problem daily. At Dunhill we came up with a solution called the 'executive briefing'. It enables you quickly to customise your CV to each specific job, and acts as a focusing device for whoever interviews you.

Like many great ideas, the executive briefing is beautiful in its simplicity. It is a sheet of paper with the company's requirements for the job opening listed on the left side, and your skills – matching point by point the company's needs – on the right.

Send an executive briefing with every CV; it will substantially increase your chances of obtaining an interview with the company. An executive briefing sent with a CV provides a comprehensive picture of a thorough professional, plus a personalised, fast and easy-to-read synopsis that details exactly how you can help with their current needs.

The use of an executive briefing is naturally restricted to jobs that you have discovered through your own efforts or seen advertised. It is obviously not appropriate for sending when the requirements of a specific job are unavailable. However, by following the directions in the next chapter, you will be able to use it frequently and effectively.

It looks like this:

Executive Briefing

Dear Sir/Madam

While my curriculum vitae will provide you with a general outline of my work history, my problem-solving abilities and some achievements, I have taken the time to list your current specific requirements and my applicable skills in those areas. I hope this will enable you to use your time effectively today.

Your Requirements:	My Skills:
1. Management of public library service area (for circulation, reference, etc).	1. Experience as head reference librarian at University of Redbrick.
2. Supervision of 14 full-time support employees.	2. Supervised support staff of 17.
3. Ability to work with larger supervisory team in planning, budgeting and policy formulating.	3. During my last year, I was responsible for budget and reformation of circulation rules.
4. ALA.	4. I have this qualification.
5. Three years' experience.	5. One year with public library; two with University of Redbrick.

This briefing ensures that each CV you send out addresses the job's specific needs and that every interviewer at that company will be interviewing you for the same job.

Part 2
Getting to Square One

With the groundwork completed, you are geared up and ready to knock 'em for six. So how do you begin?

What are your choices? Read the sits vacant ads? Everybody else does. Apply for jobs listed with the unemployment office? Everybody else does. Send CVs to companies on the off-chance they have a job that fits yours? Everybody else does. Or, of course, you can wait for someone to ring you. Employ these tactics as your main thrust for hunting down the best jobs in town, and you will fail as do *thousands* of other people who fall into the trap of using such outdated job-hunting techniques.

When you look like a penguin, act like a penguin and hide among penguins, don't be surprised if you get lost in the flock. Today's business market-place demands a different approach. Your career does not take care of itself; you must go out and grab the opportunities. Grant yourself the right to pick and choose among *many* job offers with a guaranteed approach: pick up the telephone. 'Hello, Mr Smith? My name is Martin Yate. I am an experienced training specialist...'

It's as easy as that.

Guide your destiny by speaking directly to the professionals who make their living in the same way you do. A few minutes spent phoning different companies from your research dossier, and you will have an interview. When you get one interview from making a few calls, how many do you think could be arranged with a day's concerted effort?

Because you are in control, it is possible to set your multiple interviews close together. This way your interviewing skills improve from one to the next. And soon, instead of scheduling multiple interviews, you can be weighing multiple job offers.

Chapter 4

Paint the Perfect Picture on the Phone

Before making that first, nerve-racking telephone call, you must be prepared to achieve one of these three goals. They are listed in order of priority:

- I will arrange a meeting; or
- I will arrange a time to talk further on the phone; or
- I will establish a referral lead on a promising job opening elsewhere.

Always keep these goals in mind. By the time you finish the next four chapters, you'll be able to achieve any one of them quickly and easily.

Planning the phone call

To make the initial phone call a success, all you need to do is paint a convincing word picture of yourself. To start, remember the old saying: 'No one really listens; we are all just waiting for our turn to speak.' With this in mind, you shouldn't expect to hold anyone's attention for long, so the picture you create needs to be brief yet thorough. Most of all, it should be specific enough to arouse interest, to make the company representative prick up his or her ears; vague enough to encourage questions, to make him or her *pursue* you. The aim is to paint a representation of your skills in broad brush strokes with examples of the money-making, money-saving or time-saving accomplishments all companies like to hear about.

A presentation made over the telephone must possess four characteristics to be successful. These can best be remembered by an old acronym from the advertising world, AIDA.

A – You must get the company representative's *attention.*

I – You must get the company representative's *interest.*

D – You must create a *desire* to know more about you.

A – You must encourage the company representative to take
action.

With AIDA you get noticed. The interest you generate will be
displayed by questions being asked. 'How much are you making?'
or, 'Do you have a degree?' or, 'How many years' experience do
you have?' By giving the appropriate answers to these and
other questions (which will be discussed in detail), you will change
interest into a desire to meet you and convert that desire into an
interview.

The types of question you are asked also enable you to identify
the company's specific needs, and once they are identified, you
can gear the on-going conversation towards those needs.

Here are the steps in building your AIDA presentation:

STEP 1
This covers who you are and what you do. It is planned to get the
company representative's attention, to give the person a reason
to stay on the phone. This introduction will include your job title
and a brief generalised description of your duties and responsibilities. Use a non-specific job title, as you did for your CV.
Remember: getting a foot in the door with a generalised title can
provide the occasion to sell your superior skills.

Tell just enough about yourself to whet the company's
appetite, and cause the representative to start asking questions.
Again, keep your description a little vague. For example, if you
describe yourself as simply 'experienced', the company representative *must* try to qualify your statement with a question: 'How
much experience do you have?' That way, you establish a level of
interest. *But,* if you describe yourself as having four years'
experience, and the company is looking for seven, you are likely
to be ruled out without even knowing there was a job to be filled.
Never specify exact experience or list all your accomplishments
during the initial presentation. Your aim is just to open a
dialogue. Example:

Good morning, Mr Smith. My name is Jenny Jones. I am an
experienced office equipment salesperson with an in-depth
knowledge of the office products industry. Have I caught you
at a good time?

Note. Never *ever* ask if you have caught someone at a *bad* time. You
are offering them an excuse to say 'yes'. By the same token,
asking whether you have caught someone at a good time will

usually get you a 'yes'. Then you can go directly into the rest of your presentation.

STEP 2

Now you are ready to generate interest, and from that, desire; it's time to sell one or two of your accomplishments. You should already have identified these during the CV-building exercises. Pull out no more than two items and follow your introductory sentence with them. Keep them brief and to the point, without embellishments. Example:

> As the No 3 salesperson in my company, I increased sales in my territory 15 per cent to over £1 million. In the last six months, I won three major accounts from my competitors.

STEP 3

You have made the company representative want to know more about you, so now you can make him or her take action. Include the reason for your call and a request to meet. It should be carefully constructed to finish with a question that will bring a positive response, which will launch the two of you into a nuts-and-bolts discussion between two professionals. Example:

> The reason I'm calling, Mr Smith, is that I'm looking for a new challenge, and having researched your company, I felt that we might have some areas for discussion. Are these the types of skill and accomplishment you look for in your staff?

Your presentation ends with a question that guarantees a positive response, and the conversation gets moving.

Script your presentation

Your task now is to write out a presentation using these guidelines and your work experience. Knowing exactly what you are going to say and what you wish to achieve is the only way to generate multiple interviews and multiple job offers. When your presentation is prepared and written, read it aloud to yourself, and imagine the faceless company representative at the other end of the line. Practise with a friend or spouse.

After you make the actual presentation on the phone, you'll *really* begin to work on arranging a meeting, another phone conversation or establishing a referral. There will probably be silence on the other end after your initial pitch. Be patient. The company representative needs time to digest your words. If you feel tempted to break the silence, resist; you do not want to break the person's train of thought, nor do you want the ball back in your court.

This contemplative silence may last as long as 20 seconds, but when the company representative responds, there will be only three things that can happen:

1. The company representative can agree with you and arrange a meeting.
2. The company representative can ask questions that show interest. Examples:
   - Do you have a degree?
   - How much are you earning?

   Any question, because it denotes interest, is known as a *buy signal*. And handled properly, it will enable you to arrange a meeting.
3. The company representative can raise an objection. Examples:
   - I don't need anyone like that now.
   - Send me a CV.

These objections, when handled properly, will *also* result in an interview with the company, or at least a referral to someone else who has job openings. In fact, you will frequently find that objections prove themselves to be terrific opportunities disguised as unsolvable problems.

I hope you can handle the first option with little assistance because, for obvious reasons, it doesn't get a chapter; you can go straight to Part 3. The next two chapters focus on buy signals and objections, and how to turn them into interviews.

Chapter 5
Responding to Buy Signals

With just a touch of nervous excitement you finish your presentation: 'Are these the types of skill and accomplishment you look for in your staff?' There is silence on the other end. It is broken by a question. You breathe a sigh of relief because you remember that *any* question denotes interest and is a *buy signal*.

Now conversation is a two-way street, and you are most likely to win an interview when you take responsibility for your half of the conversation. Just as the employer's questions show interest in you, your questions should show your interest in the work done at the company. By asking questions of your own in the normal course of that chat, questions usually tagged on to the end of one of your answers, you will forward the conversation. Also, these questions help you to find out what particular skills and qualities are important to each different employer. Inquisitiveness will increase your knowledge of the opportunity at hand, and that knowledge will give you the power to arrange a meeting.

The alternative is to leave all the interrogation to the employer. That will place you on the defensive and, at the end of the talk, you will be as ignorant of the real job parameters as you were at the start. And the employer will know less about you than you might want him to know.

Applying the technique of giving a short answer and finishing each reply with a question will carry your call to its logical conclusion: the interviewer will tell you the job specifics and, as that happens, you will present the relevant skills or attributes. In any conversation, the person who asks the question controls its outcome. You phoned the employer to get an interview as the first step in generating a job offer, so take control of your destiny by taking control of the conversation. Example:

Jenny Jones. Good morning, Mr Smith. My name is Jenny Jones. I am an experienced office equipment salesperson with an in-depth knowledge of the office products industry. Have I caught you at a good time? ... As the No 3 salesperson in my company, I increased sales in my territory 15 per cent to over £1 million. In the last six months, I won three major accounts from my competitors. The reason I'm calling, Mr Smith, is that I'm looking for a new challenge and, having researched your company, I felt we might have areas for discussion. Are these the types of skill and accomplishment you look for in your staff?

(Pause.)

Mr Smith. Yes, they are. What type of equipment have you been selling? *(Buy signal!)*

J. My company carries a comprehensive range, and I sell both the top and bottom of the line, according to my customers' needs. I have been noticing a considerable interest in the new multi-function machines. *(You've made it a conversation; you further it with the following ...)* Has that been your experience recently?

S. Yes, especially in the colour and acetate capability machines. *(Useful information for you.)* Do you have a degree? *(Buy signal!)*

J. Yes, I do. *(Just enough information to keep the company representative chasing you.)* I understand your company prefers graduate salespeople to deal with its more sophisticated clients. *(Your research is paying off.)*

S. Our customer base is very sophisticated, and they expect certain behaviour and competence from us. *(An inkling of the kind of person they want to hire.)* How much experience do you have? *(Buy signal!)*

J. Well, I've worked both in operations and sales, so I have a wide experience base. *(General but thorough.)* How many years of experience are you looking for? *(Turning it around, but furthering the conversation.)*

S. Ideally, four or five for the position I have in mind. *(More good information.)* How many do you have? *(Buy signal!)*

J. I have two with this company, and one and a half before that. I fit right in with your needs, don't you agree? *(How can Mr Smith say no?)*

S. Uhmmm ... what's your territory? *(Buy signal!)*

J. I cover the metropolitan area. Mr Smith, it really *does* sound as if we might have something to talk about. *(Remember, your first goal is the face-to-face interview.)* I am planning to take Thursday and Friday off at the end of the week. Can we meet then? *(Make Mr Smith decide what day he can see you, rather than whether he will see you at all.)* Which would be best for you?

S. How about Friday morning? Can you bring a CV?

Your conversation should proceed with this give-and-take. Your questions show interest, carry the conversation forward and teach you more about the company's needs. By the end of the conversation you have an interview arranged and several key areas to promote when you arrive:

- Company sees growth in multi-function machines, especially those with colour and acetate capabilities
- They want business and personal sophistication
- They ideally want four or five years' experience
- They are interested in your metropolitan contacts.

The above is a fairly simple scenario, and even though it is constructive, it doesn't show you the tricky signals that can spell disaster in your job hunt. They are *apparently* simple buy signals, yet in reality they are a part of every interviewer's arsenal called 'knock-out' questions – questions that can save the interviewer time by quickly ruling out certain types of candidate. Although these questions most frequently arise during the initial telephone conversation, they can crop up at the face-to-face interview; the answering techniques are applicable throughout the interview cycle.

Note. We all come from different backgrounds and geographical areas. I see and recognise these regional differences every day in my training job. So understand that while my answers cover correct approaches and responses, they do not attempt to capture the rich regional and personal flavour of conversation. You and I will never talk alike. So, don't learn the example answers parrot-fashion. Instead, you should take the essence of the responses and personalise them until the words fall easily from your lips.

Knock-out questions

Buy signal. 'How much are you earning/do you want?'

This is a direct question looking for a direct answer, yet it is a knock-out question. Earning either too little or too much could ruin your chances before you're given the opportunity to shine in person. There are a number of options that could serve you better than a direct answer.

- *Put yourself above the money.* 'I'm looking for a job and a company to call home. If I am the right person for you, I'm sure you'll make me a fair offer. What is the salary range for the position?'
- *Give a vague answer.* 'In the 20s. The most important things to me are the job itself and the company. What is the salary range for the position?'
- *Or you could use a technique employed by most salespeople, and answer a question with a question.* 'How much does the job pay?' It is sometimes very effective to answer a question with a question; if you don't feel yourself to be the sales type, however, you may need to practise it.

When you are pressed a second time for an exact figure, be as honest and forthright as circumstances permit. Some people (often, unfortunately, women) are underpaid for their jobs when their work is compared to that of others in similar positions. It is not a question of perception; these women in fact make less money than they should. If you have the skills for the job and you are concerned that your current low salary will eliminate you before you have the chance to show your worth, you may want to add the value of your benefits into your basic salary. If it turns out to be too much, you can then simply explain that you were including the value of your benefits. Or you could say, 'Mr Smith, my previous employers felt I was well worth the money I earned because of my skills, dedication and honesty. Were we to meet, I'm sure I could demonstrate my value and my ability to contribute to your department. You'd like an opportunity to make that evaluation, wouldn't you?'

Notice the 'wouldn't you?' at the end of the reply. A reflexive question such as this is a great conversation-forwarding technique because it encourages a positive response. Conservative use of reflexive questions can really help you to move things along. Watch the sound of your voice, though. A reflexive question can sound pleasantly conversational or pointed and accusatory; it's a case of not *what* you say, but *how* you say it. These questions are easy to create. Just add, 'wouldn't you?', 'didn't you?', 'won't you?', 'couldn't you?', 'shouldn't you?' or 'don't you?' to the end of any sentence and the interviewer will almost always answer 'yes'. You have kept the conversation alive.

Repeat the reflexive questions to yourself. They have a certain rhythm that will help you to remember them.

Buy signal. 'Do you have a degree?'

Always answer the exact question; beware of giving unrequested and possibly too much information. For example, if you have a bachelor's degree from East Anglia, your answer is 'Yes,' not 'Yes, I have a BA in fine arts from East Anglia.' Perhaps the company wants an architecture degree. Perhaps the company representative has bad feelings about East Anglia graduates. You don't want to be knocked out before you've been given the chance to prove yourself.

'Yes, I have a degree. What background are you looking for?'

You can always answer a question with a question. 'I have a diverse educational background. Ideally, what are you looking for?'

If a degree that you lack is required, strive to use the 'university of life' answer. For instance: 'My education was cut short by the necessity of earning a living at an early age. My past managers have found that my life experience and responsible attitude are *very* valuable assets to the department. Also, I am still continuing my education.'

A small proportion of the more sensitive employers are verifying educational credentials, and if yours are checked it means the employer takes such matters seriously, so an untruth or an exaggeration could cost you a job. Think hard and long before inflating your educational background.

Buy signal. 'How much experience do you have?'

Too much or too little could easily rule you out. Be careful how you answer and try to gain time. It is a vague question, and you have a right to ask for qualifications.

'Could you help me with that question?' or, 'Are you looking for overall experience or in some specific areas?' or, 'Which areas are most important to you?' Again, you answer a question with a question. The employer's response to this, while gaining you time, tells you what it takes to do the job and therefore what you have to say to get it, so take mental notes (you can even write them down, if you have time). Then give an appropriate response.

You might want to retain control of the conversation by asking another question, for example, 'The areas of expertise you require sound very interesting, and it sounds as if you have some exciting projects on hand. Exactly what projects would I be involved with in the first few months?'

After one or two buy signal questions are asked (apart from the ones mentioned, they contain no traps), you should ask for a meeting. If you simply ask, 'Would you like to meet me?' there are only two possible responses: yes or no. Your options are greatly lessened. However, when you intimate that you will be in the area on a particular date or dates ('I'm going to be in town on Thursday and Friday, Mr Smith. Which would be better for you?'), you have asked a question that moves the conversation along dramatically. This question gives the company representative the choice of meeting you on Thursday or Friday, rather than meeting you or not meeting you. By presuming the 'yes', you reduce the chances of hearing a negative, and increase the possibility of a face-to-face meeting.

Chapter 6

Responding to Objections

Even with the most convincing word picture, the silence may not be broken by a buy signal, but by an objection. An objection is usually a statement, not a question: 'Why don't you send me a CV?' or, 'I haven't time to see you,' or, 'I don't need anyone like you right now.'

These seem like brush-off lines, but almost all objections can be converted into interviews when handled properly. Often they are just disguised opportunities. As this section teaches you to seize hidden opportunities successfully, notice what all your responses have in common with buy signals: they all end with a question, a question that will enable you to learn more about the reason for the objection, overcome it and once again lead the conversation towards a face-to-face interview.

In dealing with objections, as with differences of opinion, nothing is gained by confrontation, although much is to be gained by appreciating the other person's point of view. Most objections you hear are best handled by first demonstrating your understanding of the other's viewpoint. Always start your response with 'I understand,' or, 'I can appreciate your position,' or, 'I see your point,' or, 'Of course,' followed by, 'However ...' or, 'Also consider ...' or a similar line that carries the conversation forward.

Remember, these responses should not be learned merely to be repeated. You need only to understand and implement their *meaning*, to understand their *concept* and put the answers in your own words. Personalise all the suggestions to your character and style of speech.

Objection. 'Why don't you send me a CV?'

Danger here. The company representative may be genuinely interested in seeing your CV as a first step in the interview cycle; or it may be a polite way of getting you off the phone. You should identify what the real reason is without causing antagonism. At the same time, you want to open up the conversation. A good reply would be: 'Of course, Mr Smith. Would you give me your exact title and the full address? ... Thank you. So that I can be sure that my qualifications fit your needs, what skills are you looking for in this position?'

Notice the steps:

- Apparent agreement to start
- A show of consideration
- A question to guide the conversation at the end.

Answering in this fashion will open up the conversation. Now, our hypothetical Mr Smith will relay the aspects of the job that are important to him. With this knowledge, you can sell Smith your skills over the phone. Also, you will be able to draw attention to your skills in these specific areas in the future in:

- Following conversations
- The covering letter to your CV
- The executive briefing
- Your face-to-face meeting
- Your follow-up after the meeting.

The information you glean will give you power and will increase your chances of receiving a job offer.

Objection. 'I haven't time to see you.'

If the employer is too busy to see you, he or she has a problem and, by recognising that, perhaps you can show yourself as the one to solve it. However, you should avoid confrontation; it is important that you demonstrate empathy for the speaker. Agree, empathise and ask a question that moves the conversation forward.

'I understand how busy you must be; it sounds like the kind of atmosphere I could work well in. Perhaps I could ring you back at a better time. When are you least busy – the morning or afternoon?'

The company representative will either make time to talk now, or will arrange a better time for the two of you to talk further.

Here are three other wordings you could use for the same objection: 'Since you are so busy, what is the best time of day for you? First thing in the morning, or is the afternoon a quieter time?' or, 'I will be in your area tomorrow, so why don't I come by and see you?'

Or, of course, you can combine the two: 'I'm going to be in your part of town tomorrow, and I could drop by and see you. What is your quietest time, morning or afternoon?' By presuming the invitation to a meeting, you make it harder for the company representative to object. And if he or she is *truly* busy, your consideration will make it even harder to object.

Objection. 'You are earning too much.'

You should not have brought up salary in the first place. Go straight to gaol. If the client brought up the matter, that's a buy signal, which was discussed in the last chapter. If the job really doesn't pay enough, all you've gained is experience. Avoid confrontation on the salary question too early on. How to make a success of this seeming dead end is handled in the next chapter.

Objection. 'We only promote from within.'

Your response could be: 'I realise that, Mr Smith. Your development of employees is a major reason I want to join you! I am bright, conscientious and need a company like yours. When you do recruit from outside, what assets are you looking for?'

The response finishes with a question designed to carry the conversation forward, and to give you a new opportunity to sell yourself. Notice that the response assumes that the company *is* recruiting from outside, even though the company representative has said otherwise. You have called his bluff, but in a professional, inoffensive manner.

Objection. 'You'll have to talk to personnel.'

Your reply is: 'Of course, Mr Smith. Whom should I speak to in personnel and what specific position should I mention?'

You cover a good deal of ground with this response. You establish whether there is a job there or whether you are being fobbed off to personnel to waste their time and your own. Also, you move the conversation forward again, and have changed the thrust of it to your advantage. Develop a specific job-related question to ask while the company representative is answering the first question. It can open a fruitful line for you to pursue. If you receive a non-specific reply, probe a little deeper. A simple phrase like, 'That's interesting, please tell me more,' or, 'Why's that?' will usually do the trick.

Or you can ask: 'When I speak to personnel, will it be about a specific job *you* have, or is it to see if I might fill a position elsewhere in the company?'

Armed with this information, you can talk to personnel about your conversation with Mr Smith. Remember to get the name of a specific person to speak to, and to quote the company representative. Example:

Good morning, Mr Johnson. Mr Smith, the regional sales manager, suggested we should speak to arrange an interview.

This way, you will show personnel that you are *not* a waste of their time; because you know someone in the company, you won't be regarded as one of the hundreds of blind callers they always get. As the most overworked, understaffed department in a company, they will appreciate that. Most important, you will stand out, be noticed.

Don't look at the personnel department as a roadblock; it may contain a host of opportunities for you. Because a large company may have many different departments that can use your talents, personnel is likely to be the only department that knows all the openings. You might be able to arrange three or four interviews with the same company for three or four different positions!

Objection. 'I really wanted someone with a degree.'

You could answer *this* by saying: 'Mr Smith, I appreciate your position. It was necessary that I start earning a living early in life. If we meet, I am certain you would recognise the value of my additional practical experience. All we would need is a short while, and I'm going to be in your area tomorrow and next week. When would be a good time for you?'

If that doesn't work, ask what the company policy is for support and encouragement of employees taking night classes, continuing education courses etc.

Objection. 'I don't need anyone like you now.'

Short of suggesting the employer fire someone to make room for you, the chances of getting an interview with this particular company are slim, but with the right question, this person will give you a personal introduction to someone else who could use your talents. Asking that right question or series of questions is what networking and the next chapter are all about. So on the occasions when the techniques for answering buy signals or rebutting objections do not get you a meeting, 'Getting Live Leads from Dead Ends' will!

Chapter 7
Getting Live Leads from Dead Ends

There will be times when you have said all the right things on the phone, but hear, 'I don't need anyone like you just now.' Not every company has a job opening for you, nor are you right for every job. There will be times when you must accept a temporary setback and understand that the rejection is not one of you as a human being. By using other interview development questions, though, you will be able to turn these occasions into job interviews.

The company representative is a professional and knows other professionals in his or her field, in other departments, subsidiaries, even other companies. If you approach the phone presentation in a professional manner, he or she, as a fellow professional, will be glad to advise you on who is looking for someone with your skills. Nearly everyone you call will be pleased to head you in the right direction, *but only if you ask!* And you'll be able to ask as many questions as you want, because you will be recognised as a colleague intelligently using the professional network. The company representative knows also that his good turn in referring you to a friend at another company will be returned in future. And, as a general rule, companies prefer candidates to be referred this way over any other method.

But do *not* expect people to be clairvoyant. There are two sayings:

'You get what you ask for,'

and

'If you don't ask, you don't get.'

When you are sure that no job openings exist within a particular company, *ask* one of these questions:

- Who else in the company might need someone with my qualifications?
- Does your company have any other divisions or subsidiaries that might need someone with my attributes?

- Do you know anyone in the business community who might have a lead for me?
- What are the most rapidly growing companies in the area?
- Who should I speak to there?
- Do you know anyone at the Corporation Company Limited?
- When do you anticipate an opening in your company?
- Are you planning any expansion or new projects that might create an opening?
- Do you see any change in your manpower needs?

Each one of these interview development questions can gain you an introduction or lead to a fresh opportunity. The questions have not been put in any order of importance. That is for you to do. Take a sheet of paper and, looking at the list, decide what question you would ask if you had time to ask only one. Write it down. Do this with the remaining questions on the list. As you advance, a comfortable list of questions in order of priority will be developed. Add questions of your own. For instance, the type of computer or word-processing equipment a company has might be important to some professions, but not to others, and a company representative might be able to lead you to companies that have your machines. Be sure that any question you add to your list is specific and leads to a job opening. Avoid questions like, 'How's business these days?' Time is valuable, and time is money to both of you. When you're satisfied with your list of interview development questions, put them on a fresh sheet of paper and store it safely with your telephone presentation and CV.

These interview development questions will lead you to a substantial number of jobs in the hidden job market. You are getting referrals from the 'in' crowd, who know who is recruiting whom long before that news is generally known and, by so doing, you establish a very effective referral network.

When you get leads on companies and specific individuals to talk to, be sure to thank your benefactor and ask to use his or her name as an introduction. The answer, you will find, will always be 'yes', but asking shows you as someone with manners and that *alone* will set you apart. You might also suggest to your contact that you leave your telephone number in case he or she comes across someone who can use you. You will be surprised how many people call back with a lead.

With personal permission to use someone's name on your next

networking call, you have been given the greatest of job-search gifts: a personal introduction. In these instances, your call will begin with:

> Hello, Mr Smith. My name is Jack Jones. Joseph McDonald recommended me to phone you. By the way, he sends his regards. *(Pause for any response to this.)* He felt we might have a useful discussion.

Follow up on every lead you get. Too many people become elated at securing themselves an interview and then cease all effort to generate additional interviews, believing a job offer is definitely on its way. Your goal is to have a choice of the best jobs, and without multiple interviews, there is no way you'll have that choice. Asking interview development questions ensures that you are tapping all the secret recesses of the hidden job market.
Networking is a continuous cycle:

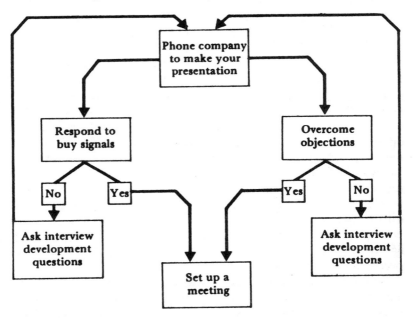

Make a commitment to sell yourself, to make telephone calls, to make a referral network, to recognise buy signals and objections for what they really are – opportunities to shine. Make a commitment to ask interview development questions at every seeming dead end: they will lead you to every job in town.

Chapter 8

The Telephone Interview

In this glorious technological age, the first contact with a potential employer is always by telephone. It's the way business is done today.

It happens in one of three ways:

- When you are networking, and the company representative goes into a screening process immediately because you have aroused his or her interest;
- A company phones unexpectedly as a result of a CV you have mailed, and catches you off-guard; or
- You, or an agency you have spoken to, have set up a specific time for a telephone interview.

Whatever circumstance creates this telephone interview, you must be prepared to handle the questioning and use every means at your disposal to win the real thing – the *face-to-face* meeting. The telephone interview is the trial run for the face-to-face, and is an opportunity not to be fumbled; your happiness and prosperity may depend on it.

This, the first contact with your future employer, will test your mental preparation. Remember: you can plant in your mind any thought, any plan, desire, strategy or purpose, and translate it into reality. Put your goal down on paper and read it aloud to yourself every day, because the constant reiteration will crystallise your aims, and that provides the most solid base of preparation.

Being prepared for a telephone interview takes organisation. You never know when a company will ring once you have started networking (the word gets around), although it is usually at the worst of times, such as 8 o'clock on Monday morning when you are sleeping late, or 4.56 in the afternoon, just as you return from walking the dog. You can avoid being caught *completely* off-guard by keeping your CV and alphabetised company dossiers by the telephone.

The most obvious (and often most neglected) point to

remember is this: during the interview, the company representative has only ears with which to judge you. This is something you must overcome. Here are some tips:

☐ *Take a surprise phone call in your stride.* If you receive a call as a result of a mailed CV or a telephone message you left, and you are unprepared, be calm. Sound positive, friendly and collected:

> Thank you for phoning, Mr McLeish. How do you spell that? Would you wait just a moment while I close the door?

Put the phone down, take three deep breaths to slow your heart down, pull out the appropriate company dossier and your CV, put a smile on your face (it improves the timbre of your voice) and pick up the phone again. Now you are in control of yourself and the situation.

☐ *Beware of over-familiarity.* You should always refer to the interviewer by his or her surname until invited to do otherwise.

☐ *Allow the company representative to do most of the talking, to ask most (but not all) of the questions.* Keep up your end of the conversation. This is, after all, a sales presentation, so be sure to ask a few questions of your own that will reveal you as an intelligent person and provide you with the opportunity to promote your candidacy. For example, ask what immediate projects the interviewer's department is involved in, or the biggest challenges that are being tackled. When the interviewer answers your questions, you will either have a clear picture of how to sell yourself, or you will ask a follow-up question for clarification. For example: 'What specific skills and personality traits do you think are necessary for a person to succeed with those challenges?' Everyone employs a problem-solver – find the problem and you are already halfway towards the offer.

☐ *Beware of giving yes/no answers.* They give no real information about your abilities.

☐ *Be factual in your answers.* Brief yet thorough.

☐ *Speak directly into the telephone.* Keep the mouthpiece about 1 inch from your mouth. Do not smoke or eat while on the phone. Numbered among the mystical properties of our telephone system is its excellence at picking up and amplifying background music and voices, especially young ones. This is only excelled by the power with which it transmits the sounds of food being chewed or smoke being inhaled or exhaled. Smokers, remember:

there are no laws about discriminating against smokers, and therefore all non-smokers naturally discriminate. They know that even if you don't smoke at the interview, you'll have been chain-smoking before and will carry the smell with you as long as you are around them. So, they won't even give you a chance to get through the door.

☐ *Take notes.* They will be invaluable to you in preparing for the face-to-face meeting. If, for any reason, the company representative is interrupted, jot down the topic under discussion. When he or she gets back on the line, you helpfully recap: 'We were just discussing . . .' This will be appreciated, and will set you apart from the others.

The company representative may talk about the organisation, and, from the dossier in front of you, you will also know facts about the set-up. A little flattery goes a long way: admire the company's achievements and you are, in fact, admiring the interviewer. Likewise, if any areas of common interest arise, comment on them, and agree with the interviewer when it is possible; people engage people like themselves.

If the interviewer does not give you the openings you need to sell yourself, be ready to salvage the situation and turn it to your advantage. Have a few work-related questions prepared (eg 'What exactly will be the three major responsibilities in this job?' or, 'Would I be using a personal computer?'). While you are getting the explanation, wait for a pause so that you can tell the interviewer your appropriate skills: 'Would it be of value if I described my experience in the area of office management?' or, 'Then my experience in word processing should be a great help to you.' Under no circumstances, though, should you ask about the money you want or benefits and holidays; that comes later.

Remember that your single objective at this point is to sell yourself and your skills; if you don't do that, you may never get the face-to-face interview.

The telephone interview has come to an end when you are asked whether you have any questions. Ask any more questions that will improve your understanding of the job requirements. If you haven't asked before, now is the time to establish what projects you would be working on in the first six months. By discovering them now, you will have time before the face-to-face meeting to package your skills to the needs at hand, and to create the appropriate executive briefing.

And if you have not already asked or been invited to meet the interviewer, now is the time. Take the initiative.

'It sounds like a very interesting opportunity, Ms/Mr Smith, and a situation where I could definitely make a contribution. The most pressing question I have now is, when can we meet?' (*Note.* Even though the emphasis throughout has been on putting things in your own words, *do* use 'make a contribution'. It shows pride in your work – a key personal trait.)

Once the details are confirmed, finish with this request: 'If I need any additional information before the interview, I would like to feel free to get back to you.' The company representative will naturally agree. No matter how many questions have been answered in the initial conversation, there will always be something you forget. This allows you to phone again to satisfy any curiosity and will also enable you to increase rapport. Don't take *too* much advantage of this, though. One well-placed phone call that contains two or three considered questions will be appreciated; four or five phone calls will not.

Taking care to ascertain the correct spelling and pronunciation of the interviewer's name shows your concern for the small but important things in life: it *will* be noticed. This is also a good time to establish who else will be interviewing you, their titles and how long the meeting is expected to last. Follow with a casual enquiry as to what direction the meeting will take.

'Can you tell me some of the critical areas we will discuss on Thursday?' you might ask. The knowledge gained will go a long way in packaging yourself and will allow you time to brush up any weak or rusty areas.

It is difficult to evaluate an opportunity properly over the telephone. Even if the job doesn't sound right, go to the interview. It will give you practice, and the job may look better when you have more facts. You might even discover a more suitable opening when you go to the face-to-face interview.

Chapter 9

The Curtain Goes Up

Backstage in the theatre, the announcement, 'Places, please', is made five minutes before the curtain goes up. This is the performers' signal to psych themselves up, complete final costume adjustments and make time to reach the stage. They are getting ready to go on stage and knock 'em dead. You should go through a similar process.

Winning that job offer depends not only on the things you do well, but also on the absence of things you do poorly. As the interview date approaches, settle down with your CV and the exercises you performed in building it. Immerse yourself in your past successes and strengths. This is a time for building confidence. A little nervousness is perfectly natural and healthy, but channel the extra energy in a positive direction by beginning your physical and mental preparations. First, you should assemble your interview kit. It will include:

☐ *The company dossier.*

☐ *Two or three copies of your curriculum vitae, all but one for the interviewer.* It is perfectly all right to have it in front of you at the interview; it shows you are organised. It also makes a great cheat sheet (after all, the interviewer is using it for that reason) and it can be kept on your lap during the interview with pad and pencil. It is not unusual to hear, 'Mr Jones wasn't made an offer because he didn't pay attention to detail and could not even remember his employment dates.' And those are just the kinds of thing you are likely to forget in the heat of the moment.

☐ *A pad of paper and writing instruments.* These articles have a twofold purpose. They demonstrate your organisation and interest in the job; they also give you something constructive to do with your hands during the interview. Bring along a blue or black pen for filling in applications.

☐ *Contact telephone numbers.* If you are detained on the way to the interview, you can ring and let the company representative know.

☐ *Take the sensible precaution of gathering reference letters from your employers, just in case.*

☐ *A list of job-related questions.* During the interview is the time when you gather information to evaluate a job (the actual evaluation comes when you have an offer in hand). At the end of the interview, you will be given the opportunity to ask additional questions. Develop some that help you to understand the job's parameters and potential. You might ask:

- Why is the job open?
- Where does the job lead?
- What is the job's relationship to other departments?
- How do the job and the department relate to corporate aims?

For a longer list of questions that it might be valuable to ask along these lines, see Chapter 19, 'Negotiating the Offer'. Understand, though, that some will obviously only be appropriate in the context of serious negotiation. You can also find good questions to ask in the answer to 'Do you have any questions?' on page 81.

Now you have a little more work to do:

☐ *Gather any additional information you can about the company or the job.* If time permits, ask the interviewer's secretary to send you some company literature. Absorb whatever you can.

☐ *Make sure you have directions for reaching the venue.* Decide on your form of transport and finalise your time of departure. Check the route, distance and travel time. Write all this down legibly and put it with the rest of your interview kit. If you forget to verify date, time and place, you might not even arrive at the right place, or on the right day, for your interview.

Personal appearance

First impressions are the strongest you make, and they are based on your appearance. There is only one way to dress for the first meeting: clean-cut and conservative. You may or may not see yourself this way, but how you see yourself is not important now; your only concern is how others see you. As you could be asked to appear for an interview at a scant couple of hours' notice, you must be in a constant state of readiness. Keep your best two suits of clothing freshly cleaned, shirts ironed and shoes polished. Never wear these outfits unless you are being interviewed. Here are some more tips:

- Regardless of sex or hairstyle, have your hair trimmed once a month.
- Keep jewellery to a minimum. A wedding or signet ring is acceptable, of course.
- While a shower or bath prior to an interview is most desirable, the wearing of aftershave or perfume is most decidedly not. You are trying to be appointed, not dated.
- You should never drink alcohol the day before an interview. It affects your eyes, your skin and your wits.
- Nails should be trimmed and manicured at all times, even if you work with your hands.

For women:

- Wear a suit or a dress with a jacket. Do not wear a trouser suit or jeans.
- If you carry a briefcase, don't carry a handbag as well. You may meet a number of people and will have trouble juggling your luggage to shake hands.
- Wear low heels. Spike heels make you wobble and are regarded by many as inappropriate in the workplace.
- Avoid linen; it creases too easily.
- Stay away from anything low-cut, tight or diaphanous.

For men:

- Avoid loud colours and anything that has been faddish...
- ... such as that dayglo tie. A 2½ to 2¾ inch tie is *de rigueur*. Patterns should be paisley or foulard. Avoid anything wider unless you are applying for a job as a carpet salesman.
- Blue or grey for suits primarily. White for shirts is always safest.
- Black shoes with plain socks.

The way you dress, the way you look to a potential employer at the first interview, tells him or her how you feel about yourself. It also portrays how seriously you take both the interview and the interviewer.

Arrival

To arrive at an interview too early indicates over-anxiousness; to arrive late is inconsiderate. The only sensible solution is to arrive at the interview on time, but at the location early. This allows you time to visit the wash room and make the necessary adjustments to your appearance. Take a couple of minutes in this temporary sanctuary to perform your final mental preparations:

- Review the company dossier.
- Recall the positive things you will say about past employers.
- Breathe deeply and slowly for a minute. This will dispel your natural physical tension.
- Repeat to yourself that the interview will be a success and afterwards the company representatives will wonder how they ever managed without you.
- Smile and head for the interview.

Under no circumstances back out because you do not like the receptionist or the look of the office; that would be allowing interview nerves to get the better of you. As you are shown into the office, you are on!

This potential new employer wants an aggressive and dynamic employee, but someone who is less aggressive and dynamic than himself, so take your lead from the interviewer.

Do:

- Give a firm handshake; once is enough.
- Make eye contact and smile. Say, 'Hello, Ms Smith. I am John Jones. I have been looking forward to meeting you.'

Do not:

- Use first names (unless asked).
- Smoke (even if invited).
- Sit down (until invited).
- Show anxiety or boredom.
- Look at your watch.
- Discuss equal rights, sex, race, national origin, religion, age.
- Show samples of your work (unless requested).
- Ask about benefits, salary, holidays.
- Assume a submissive role; treat the interviewer with respect, but as an equal.

Now you are ready for anything. Except for the tough questions that are going to be thrown at you next.

Part 3
Great Answers to Tough Interview Questions

'Like being on trial for your life' is how many people look at a job interview. They are probably right. With the interviewer as judge and jury, you are at least on trial for your livelihood. Therefore, you must lay the foundation for a winning defence. F Lee Bailey, America's most celebrated defence lawyer, attributes his success in the court-room to preparation. He likens himself to a magician going into court with 50 rabbits in his hat, not knowing which one he'll really need, and ready to pull out any single one. Bailey is successful because he is ready for any eventuality. He takes the time to analyse every situation and every possible option. He never underestimates his opposition. He is always prepared. F Lee Bailey usually wins.

Another famous lawyer, Louis Nizer, successfully defended *all* of his 50-plus capital charge clients. When praised as the greatest court-room performer of his day, Nizer denied the accolade. He claimed for himself the distinction of being the *best prepared*.

You won't win your day in court just on your skills. As competition for the best jobs increases, employers are comparing more and more applicants for every opening and asking more and more questions. To win against stiff competition, you need more than just your merits. When the race is close, the final winner is often as not picked for a comparative lack of negatives when ranged against the other contenders. Like Bailey and Nizer, you can prove to yourself that the job always goes to the best prepared.

During an interview, employers ask you dozens of searching questions: questions that test your confidence, poise and desirable personality traits; questions that trick you into contradicting yourself, and questions that probe your quick thinking and job skills. They are all designed so that the interviewer can make decisions in four critical areas:

- Can you do the job?
- Do you fit the company image?

- Will you complement or disrupt the department?
- Is the money right?

Notice that only one of the critical areas has anything to do with your professional skills. Being able to do the job is only part-way to getting an offer. Whether you will fit in and make a contribution is just as important to the interviewer. Those traits the company probes for during the interview are the same that will mark a person for professional growth when on board. In this era of high unemployment and high specialisation, companies become more critical in the selection process and look more actively for certain traits, some of which cannot be ascertained by a direct question or answer. Consequently, the interviewer will seek a pattern in your replies that shows your possession of these traits.

The time spent in 'court' on trial for your livelihood contains four deadly traps:

- Failure to listen to the question.
- Annoying the interviewer by answering a question that was not asked.
- Providing superfluous information (keep answers brief, thorough, and to the point).
- Attempting to interview without preparation.

The effect of these blunders is cumulative, and each reduces your chances of receiving a job offer.

The number of offers you win in your search for the ideal job depends on your ability to answer a staggering array of questions in terms that have value and relevance to the employer: 'Why do you want to work here?' or, 'What are your biggest accomplishments?' or, 'How long will it take you to make a contribution?' or, 'Why should I take you on?' or, 'What can you do for us that someone else cannot do?' or, 'What is your greatest weakness?' or, 'Why aren't you earning more?' or, 'What interests you least about this job?' are just *some* of the questions you will be asked.

The specimen answers in the following chapters come from across the job spectrum. While the specimen answer might come from the mouth of an administrator – and you are a salesperson – the common denominator of all job functions in contributing to the bottom line will help you draw the parallel to *your* job.

You will also notice that each of the specimen answers teaches a small, yet valuable lesson in good business behaviour; something you can use both to get the job and to make a good impression when you are on board.

And remember, the answers provided in the following chapters should not be repeated word for word, exactly as they come off the page. *You* have your own style of speech (not to mention your own kind of business experience), so try to put the answers in your *own* words.

Chapter 10

How to Knock 'em for Six

☐ *Describe a situation where your work or one of your ideas was criticised.*
☐ *Have you done the best work you are capable of doing?*
☐ *What problems do you have getting along with others?*
☐ *How long will you stay with the company?*
☐ *I'm not sure you're suitable for the job.*
☐ *Tell me about something you are not very proud of.*
☐ *What are some of the things your manager did that you disliked?*
☐ *What aspects of your job do you consider most crucial?*

Can you answer all these questions off the top of your head? Can you do it in a way that will set your worth above the other job candidates? I doubt it; they were *designed* to catch you off guard. But they won't after you have read this book.

Even if you could answer some of them, it would not be enough to assure you of victory: the employer is looking for certain intangible assets as well. Think back to your last job for a moment. Can you recall someone with fewer skills, less professionalism and less dedication who somehow levered his or her career into a position of superiority to yours? He or she was able to do this only by cleverly projecting a series of personality traits that are universally sought by all successful companies. Building these key traits into your answers to the interviewer's questions will win you any job and set the stage for your career growth at the new company.

There are 20 key personality traits; they are the passport to your success at an interview. Use them for reference as you customise your answers to this chapter's tough questions.

Personal profile

Personal profile keys are searched for by the interviewer to determine what type of person you *really* are. The presence of these keys in your answers tells the company representative how you feel about yourself, your chosen career and what you will be like to work with. Few of these keys will arise from direct questions. Your future employer will be searching for them in your answers to specific job performance probes. The following words and phrases are those you will project as part of your successful, healthy personal profile:

- *Drive*. A desire to get things done. Goal-oriented.
- *Motivation*. Enthusiasm and a willingness to ask questions. A company realises that a motivated person accepts added challenges and does that little bit extra on every job.
- *Communication skills*. More than ever, the ability to talk and write effectively to people at all levels in a company is a key to success.
- *Chemistry*. The company representative is looking for someone who does not get rattled, wears a smile, is confident without self-importance, gets along with others; who is, in short, a team player.
- *Energy*. Someone who always gives that extra effort in the little things as well as important matters.
- *Determination*. Someone who does not back off when a problem or situation gets tough.
- *Confidence*. Not braggadocio. Poise. Friendly, honest and open with all employees, high or low. Neither intimidated by the top brass, nor overly familiar.

Professional profile

All companies seek employees who respect their profession and their employer. Projecting these professional traits will identify you as loyal, reliable and trustworthy:

- *Reliability*. Following up on yourself, not relying on anyone else to ensure that the job is well done, and keeping management informed every step of the way.
- *Honesty/Integrity*. Taking responsibility for your actions, both good and bad. Always making decisions in the best interests of the company, never on whim or personal preference.
- *Pride*. Pride in a job well done. Always taking the extra step to make sure that the job is done to the best of your ability. Paying attention to the details.
- *Dedication*. Whatever it takes in time and effort to see a project through to completion, on deadline.
- *Analytical skills*. Weighing the pros and cons. Not jumping at the first solution to a problem that presents itself. The

short- and long-term benefits of a solution against all its possible negatives.
- *Listening skills*. Listening and understanding, as opposed to waiting your turn to speak.

Achievement profile

I mentioned earlier that companies have very limited interests: making money, saving money (the same as making money) and saving time, which does both. Projecting your achievement profile, in however humble a fashion, is the key to winning any job.

- *Money saved*. Every penny saved by your thought and efficiency is a penny earned for the company.
- *Time saved*. Every moment saved by your thought and efficiency enables your company to save money and make more in the additional time available. Double bonus.
- *Money earned*. Generating revenue is the goal of every company.

Business profile

Projecting your business profile is important on those occasions when you cannot demonstrate ways you have made money, saved money or saved time for previous employers. These keys demonstrate that you are always on the look-out for opportunities to contribute, and that you keep your boss informed when an opportunity arises.

- *Efficiency*. Always keep an eye open for wastage of time, effort, resources and money.
- *Economy*. Most problems have two solutions: an expensive one, and one that the company would prefer to implement.
- *Procedures*. Procedures exist to keep the company profitable. Don't work around them. This also means keeping your boss informed. You tell your boss about problems or good ideas, not his or her boss. Follow the chain of command. Do not implement your own 'improved' procedures or organise others to do so.
- *Profit*. The reason all the above traits are so universally admired in the business world is because they relate to profit.

Stress how your qualifications match the job requirements

As the requirements of the job are unfolded for you at the interview, meet them point by point with your qualifications. If your experience is limited, stress the key profile traits, your relevant interests and desire to learn. If you are weak in just one particular area, keep your mouth shut; perhaps that dimension will not arise. If the area is probed, be prepared to handle and overcome the negative by stressing additional complementary skills that compensate.

Do not show discouragement if the interview appears to be going poorly. You have nothing to gain by showing defeat, and it could merely be an interview tactic to test your self-confidence.

If for any reason you get flustered or lost, keep a straight face and posture; gain time to marshal your thoughts by asking, 'Could you help me with that?' or, 'Would you repeat that?' or, 'That's a good question; I want to be sure I understand. Could you please explain that again?'

The tough questions

Now it is time for you to study the tough questions. Use the examples and explanations to build answers that promote your background and skills.

□ *What are the reasons for your success in this profession?*

With this question, the interviewer is not interested in examples of your success – he wants to know what makes you tick. Keep your answers short, general and to the point. Using your work experience, personalise and use value keys from your personal profile, professional profile and business profile. For example, 'I attribute my success to three reasons: the support I've always received from co-workers, which always encourages me to be cooperative and look at my specific job in terms of what we as a department are trying to achieve. This gives me great pride in my work and its contribution to the department's efforts. Finally, I find that every job has its problems, and while there's always a costly solution, there's usually an economical one as well, whether it's in terms of time or money.' Then give an example from your experience that illustrates those points.

□ *What is your energy level like? Describe a typical day.*

You must demonstrate good use of your time, that you believe in planning your day beforehand, and that when it is over, you review your own performance to make sure you are reaching the desired goals. No one wants a part-time employee, so you should sell your energy level. For example, your answer might end up with: 'At the end of the day when I'm ready to go, I make a rule always to type one more letter [make one more call etc], and clear my desk for the next day.'

☐ *Why do you want to work here?*

To answer this question, you must have researched the company and built a dossier. Your research work from Chapter 1 is now rewarded. You should reply with the company's attributes as you see them. Cap your answer with reference to your belief that this can provide you with a stable and happy work environment – the interviewer's company has that reputation – and that such an atmosphere would encourage your best work.

'I'm not looking for just a pay cheque. I enjoy my work and am proud of my profession. Your company produces a superior product. I think that gives us certain things in common, and means I would fit in well with your team.'

☐ *What kind of experience do you have for this job?*

This is a golden opportunity to sell yourself but, before you do, be sure you know what is most critical to the interviewer. He or she is not just looking for a competent engineer, typist or salesperson, but for someone who can contribute quickly to the current projects. When interviewing, companies invariably give everyone a broad picture of the job, but the person they hire will be a problem-solver, someone who can contribute to the specific projects in the first six months. Only by asking will you identify the areas of your interviewer's greatest urgency and therefore interest.

If you do not know the projects you will be involved with in the first six months, you must ask. Level-headedness and analytical ability are respected, and you will naturally answer the question more appropriately. For example, a company experiencing slippage problems might appreciate this answer: 'My high-speed machining background and familiarity with your equipment will allow me to contribute quickly. I understand deadlines, delivery schedules and the importance of getting the product despatched quickly. Finally, my awareness of economy and profit has always kept reject parts to a bare minimum.'

□ *What are the broad responsibilities of a [eg] systems analyst?*

This is suddenly becoming a very popular question with interviewers, and rightly so. There are three layers to it. First, it acknowledges that all employees nowadays are required to be more efficiency- and profit-conscious, and need to know how individual responsibilities fit into the big picture. Second, the answer provides some idea of how much you will have to be taught or reoriented if and when you join the company. Third, it is a very effective knock-out question – if you lack a comprehensive understanding of your job, that's it. You'll be knocked out then and there.

While your answer must reflect an understanding of the responsibilities, be wary of falling foul of differing corporate jargon. A systems analyst in one company, for instance, may be only a programmer trainee in another. With that in mind, you may wish to preface your answer with, 'While the responsibilities of my job title vary somewhat from company to company, at my current/last job, my responsibilities included . . .' Then, in case you unwittingly trip yourself up in the answer, finish with a question: 'Which areas of relevant expertise haven't I covered?' This will give you the opportunity to recoup any mistakes.

□ *Describe how your job relates to the overall goals of your department and company.*

This probes not only your understanding of department and corporate missions, but also obliquely checks your ability to function as a team member to get the work done. Consequently, whatever the specifics of your answer, include words to this effect: 'The quality of my work directly affects the ability of others to do their work properly. As a team member, one has to be aware of the other players'

□ *What aspects of your job do you consider most crucial?*

A wrong answer can knock you out of the running in short order. The salesperson who describes expense reports as the job's most crucial aspect is a case in point. The question is designed to determine time management, prioritisation skills and any inclination for task avoidance.

□ *Are you willing to go where the company sends you?*

Unfortunately, with this one you are, as the saying goes, 'damned if you do and damned if you don't'. What is the *real* question? Do they want you to relocate or just travel on business? If you simply answer 'no', you will not get the job offer, but if you answer 'yes', you could end up in John o'Groats. So play for time and ask, 'Are you talking about business travel, or is the company relocating?' In the final analysis, your answer should be 'yes'. You don't have to accept the job, but without the offer you have no decision to make. Your single goal at an interview is to sell yourself and win a job offer. Never forget, only when you have the offer is there a decision to make.

☐ *What did you like/dislike about your last job?*

Most interviews start with a preamble by the interviewer about his company. Pay attention: this information will help you answer the question. In fact, any statement the interviewer makes about the job or corporation can be used to your advantage.

So in answer, you liked everything about your last job. You might even say your company taught you the importance of certain keys from the business profile, achievement profile or professional profile. Criticising a previous employer is a warning flag that you could be a problem employee. No one intentionally takes trouble on board, and that is what's behind the question. Keep your answers short and positive. You are only allowed one negative about past employers, and only then if your interviewer has a 'hot button' about his department or company; if so, you will have written it down on your notepad, in which case the only thing your past employer could not offer was, for example: 'The ability to contribute more in different areas in the smaller environment you have here. I really liked everything about the job. The reason I want to leave is to find a position where I can make a greater contribution. You see, I work for a big company that is encouraging increasing specialisation of skills. The smaller environment you have here will, as I said, allow me to contribute far more in different areas.' Tell them what they want to hear; replay the hot button.

Of course, if you interview with a large company, turn it around. 'I work for a small company and don't get the time to specialise in one or two major areas ...' Then replay the hot button.

☐ *What is the least relevant job you have held?*

If your least relevant job is not on your CV, it shouldn't be mentioned. Some people skip over those six months between jobs when they worked as hamburger bar counterhands just to pay the bills, and would rather not talk about it, until they hear a question like this. But a mention of a job that, according to all chronological records, you never had, will throw your integrity into question and your candidacy out the door.

Apart from that, no job in your profession has been a waste of time if it increases your knowledge about how the business works and makes money. Your answer will include: 'Every job I've held has given me new insights into my profession, and the higher one climbs, the more important the understanding of the lower-level, more menial jobs. They all play a role in making the company profitable. And anyway, it's certainly easier to schedule and plan work when you have first-hand knowledge of what others will have to do to complete their tasks.'

☐ *What have you learned from jobs you have held?*

Tie your answer to your business and professional profile. The interviewer needs to understand that you seek and can accept constructive advice, and that your business decisions are based on the ultimate good of the company, not your personal whim or preference. 'More than anything, I have learned that what is good for the company is good for me. So I listen very carefully to directions and always keep my boss informed of my actions.'

☐ *How do you feel about your progress to date?*

This question is not geared solely to rate your progress; it also rates your self-esteem (personal profile keys). Be positive, yet do not give the impression that you have already done your best work. Make the interviewer believe you see each day as an opportunity to learn and contribute, and that you see the environment at this company as conducive to your best efforts.

'Given the parameters of my job, my progress has been excellent. I know the work and understand the importance of the role it plays within my company's operations. I feel I am just reaching that point in my career when I can make significant contributions.'

☐ *Have you done the best work you are capable of doing?*

Say 'yes', and the interviewer will think you're a has-been. As with all these questions, personalise your work history and include the essence of this reply: 'I'm proud of my professional achievements to date, but I believe the best is yet to come. I am always motivated to give my best efforts, and in this job there are always opportunities to contribute when you stay alert.'

☐ *How long would you stay with the company?*

The interviewer might be thinking of offering you a job. So you must encourage him or her to sell you the job. With a tricky question like this, end your answer with a question of your own that really puts the ball back in the interviewer's court. Your reply might be: 'I would really like to settle down with this company. I take direction well and enjoy learning. As long as I am growing professionally, there is no reason for me to make a move. How long do you think I would be happy here?'

☐ *How long would it take you to make a contribution to our company?*

Again, be sure to qualify the question. In what area does the interviewer need rapid contributions? You are best advised to answer this question with a question: 'That is an excellent question. To help me answer, what do you anticipate my responsibilities will be for the first six or seven months?' You give yourself time to think while the interviewer concentrates on images of you working for the company. When your time comes to answer, start with: 'Let's say I started on Monday the 17th. It will take me a few weeks to settle down and learn the ropes. I'll be earning my keep very quickly, but making a real contribution ... (*hesitant pause*) ... Do you have a special project in mind you will want me to get involved with?' This response could lead directly to a job offer but, if not, you already have the interviewer thinking of you as an employee.

☐ *What would you like to be doing five years from now?*

The safest answer contains a desire to be regarded as a true professional and team player. As far as promotion is concerned, that depends on finding a manager with whom you can grow. Of course, you will ask what opportunities exist within the company before being any more specific: 'From what I know and what you have told me about the growth here, it seems that manufacturing is where the heavy emphasis is going to be. It seems that's where you need the effort and where I could contribute most towards the company's goals.' Or, 'I have always felt that first-hand knowledge and experience open up opportunities that one might never have considered, so while at this time I plan to be a part of [eg] manufacturing, it is reasonable to expect that other exciting opportunities will crop up in the meantime.'

71

☐ *What are your qualifications?*

Be sure you don't answer the wrong question. Does the interviewer want job-related or academic qualifications? Ask. If he or she is looking for job qualifications, you need to know exactly the work you'll be doing in the first few months. Again, notice the importance of understanding the current projects and therefore the problems that need to be tackled. Ask. Then use appropriate value keys from all four categories tied in with relevant skills and achievements. You might say: 'I can give you a general answer, but I feel my answer might be more valuable if you could tell me about specific work assignments in the early months...'

Or: 'If the major task right now is reducing the reject ratio, I should tell you this. I work in a high-speed manufacturing environment and, since I've been there, I've reduced rejects by 26 per cent...'

☐ *What are your biggest accomplishments?*

Keep your answers job-related; from earlier exercises, a number of achievements should spring to mind. If you exaggerate contributions to major projects, you will be accused of suffering from 'coffee machine syndrome', the affliction of a junior clerk who claimed success for an Apollo space mission based on his relationships with certain scientists, established at the coffee machine. You might begin your reply with: 'Although I feel my biggest achievements are still ahead of me, I am proud of my involvement with ... I made my contribution as part of that team and learned a lot in the process. We did it with hard work, concentration and an eye for the bottom line.'

☐ *How do you organise and plan for major projects?*

Effective planning requires both forward thinking ('Who and what am I going to need to get this job done?') and backward thinking ('If this job must be completed by the 20th, what steps have to be taken, and at what time, to achieve this?'). Effective planning also includes contingencies and budgets for time and cost overruns. Show that you cover all the bases.

☐ *How many hours a week do you find it necessary to work to get your job done?*

No absolutely correct answer here, so again, you have to cover all the bases. Some managers pride themselves on working nights and weekends, or on never taking their full vacation quota. Others pride themselves on their excellent planning and time management that allows them never to work more than regular office hours. You must pick the best of both worlds: 'I try to plan my time effectively and usually can. Our business always has its rushes, though, so I put in whatever effort it takes to get the job finished.' It is rare that the interviewer will then come back and ask for a specific number of hours. If that does happen, turn the question around: 'It depends on the projects. What is typical in your department?' The answer will give you the right cue, of course.

☐ *Tell me how you moved up through the organisation.*

A fast-track question, the answer to which tells a lot about your personality, your goals, your past, your future, and whether you still have any steam left in you. The answer might be long, but try to avoid rambling. Include a fair sprinkling of your key personality traits in your stories (because this is the perfect time to do it). As well as listing the promotions, you will want to demonstrate that they came as a result of dedicated, long-term effort, substantial contributions and flashes of genius.

☐ *Can you work under pressure?*

You might be tempted to give a simple yes or no answer, but don't. It reveals nothing and you lose the opportunity to sell your skills and value profiles. Actually, this common question often comes from an unskilled interviewer, because it is closed-ended. (How to handle different types of interviewer is handled in Chapter 12.) As such, it does not give you the chance to elaborate. Whenever you are asked one of these, mentally add: 'Please give me a brief yet comprehensive answer.' Do this, and you will give the information requested and seize an opportunity to sell yourself. For example, you could say: 'Yes, I usually find it stimulating. However, I believe in planning and proper management of my time to reduce panic deadlines within my area of responsibility.'

☐ *What is your greatest strength?*

Isolate high points from your background and build in a couple of the key value profiles from different categories. You will want to demonstrate pride, reliability, ability to stick with a difficult task yet change courses rapidly when required. You can rearrange the previous answer here. Your answer in part might be: 'I believe in

73

planning and proper management of my time. And yet I can still work under pressure.'

☐ *What are your outstanding qualities?*

This is essentially the same as an interviewer asking you what your greatest strengths are. While in the former question you might choose to pay attention to job-specific skills, this question asks you to talk about your personality profile. Now while you are fortunate enough to have a list of the business world's most desirable personality traits at the beginning of this chapter, try to do more than just list them. In fact, rather than offering a long 'laundry list', you might consider picking out just two or three and giving an illustration of each.

☐ *What interests you most about this job?*

Be straightforward, unless you haven't been given adequate information to determine an answer, in which case you should ask a question of your own to clarify. Perhaps you could say, 'Before I answer, could you tell me a little more about the role this job plays in the departmental goals?' or, 'Where is the biggest vacuum in your department at the moment?' The additional information you gather with these questions provides the appropriate slant to your answer: that is, what is of greatest benefit to the department and to the company. Careerwise, this obviously has the greatest benefit to you, too. Your answer then displays the personality traits that support the existing need. Your answer in part might include: 'I'm looking for a challenge and an opportunity to make a contribution, so if you feel the biggest challenge in the department is ... I'm the one for the job.' Then include the personality traits that support your statements. Perhaps: 'I like a challenge, my background demonstrates excellent problem-solving abilities, and I always see a project through to the finish.'

☐ *What are you looking for in your next job?*

You want a company where your personal profile keys and professional profile keys will allow you to contribute to business value keys. Avoid saying what you want the company to give you; you must say what you want in terms of what *you* can give to your employer. The key word in the following example is 'contribution': 'My experience at the XYZ Company has shown me I have a talent for motivating people. This is demonstrated by my team's absenteeism dropping 20 per cent, turnover steadying at 10 per cent and production increasing 12 per cent. I am looking for an opportunity to continue that kind of contribution, and a company and supervisor who will help me to develop in a professional manner.'

□ *Why should I hire you?*

Your answer will be short and to the point. It will highlight areas from your background that relate to current needs and problems. Recap the interviewer's description of the job, meeting it point by point with your skills. Finish your answer with: 'I have qualifications, I'm a team player, I take direction and have the desire to make a thorough success.'

□ *What can you do for us that someone else cannot do?*

This question will come only after a full explanation of the job has been given. Recap the interviewer's job description, then follow with: 'I can bring to this job a determination to see projects through to a proper conclusion. I listen and take direction well. I am analytical and don't jump to conclusions. And finally, I understand we are in business to make a profit, so I keep an eye on cost and return. How do these qualifications fit your needs?'

You finish with a question that asks for feedback or a powerful answer. If you haven't covered the interviewer's hot buttons, he or she will cover them now, and you can respond accordingly.

□ *Describe a difficult problem you've had to deal with.*

This is a favourite tough question. It is designed to probe your professional profile – specifically, your analytical skills: 'Well, I always follow a five-step format with a difficult problem. One, I stand back and examine the problem. Two, I recognise the problem as the symptom of other, perhaps hidden, factors. Three, I make a list of possible solutions to the problem. Four, I weigh both the consequences and cost of each solution, and determine the best solution. And five, I go to my boss, outline the problem, make my recommendation, and ask for my superior's advice and approval.'

Then give an example of a problem and your solution. For example: 'When I joined my present company, I filled the shoes of a manager who had been fired. Staff turnover was very high. My job was to reduce the turnover, improve morale and increase sales. Sales of our new copier had slumped for the fourth quarter in a row. The new employer was very concerned, and he even gave me permission to replace all the staff. The cause of the problem? The sales team had never had any sales training. All my people needed was an intensive sales training course. My boss gave me permission to join the Institute of Training and Development, which cost £70. With what I learned there, I turned the department around. Sales continued to slump in my first quarter. Then they skyrocketed. Management was pleased with the sales, my boss was pleased because the solution was effective and cheap. I only had to replace two salespeople.'

☐ *What would your references say?*

You have nothing to lose by being positive. If you demonstrate how well you and your boss got along, the interviewer does not have to ask, 'What do you dislike about your current manager?'

It is a good idea to ask past employers to give you a letter of recommendation. This way you know what is being said. It reduces the chances of the company representative checking up on you, and if you are asked this question you can pull out a sheaf of rousing accolades and hand them over.

☐ *Can we check your references?*

This question is frequently asked as a stress question to catch the over-confident candidate off guard. It is also one that is occasionally asked in the general course of events. Very few managers or companies ever check references – astounding, yet it's a fact of life. On the other hand, the higher up the corporate ladder you go, the more likely it is that your references will be checked.

There is only one answer to this question if you ever expect to get an offer: 'Yes.' Your answer may include: 'Yes, of course you can check my references. However, at present, I would like to keep matters confidential, until we have established a serious mutual interest [ie an offer]. At such time I will be pleased to furnish you with whatever references you need from previous employers. I would expect you not to approach my current employer until you have extended an offer in writing, I have accepted, we have agreed upon a start date, and I have had the opportunity to resign in a professional manner.' You are under no obligation to give references from a current employer until you have a written offer in hand. You are also well within your rights to request that references from a current employer wait until you have started your new job.

☐ *What type of decisions did you make in your last job?*

Your answer should include reference to the fact that your

decisions were all based on appropriate business profile keys. The interviewer may be searching to define your responsibilities or he or she may want to know that you don't overstep yourself. It is also an opportunity, however humble your position, to show your achievement profile.

For example: 'Being in charge of the post room, I am responsible for making sure people get information without delay. The job is well defined, and my decisions aren't that difficult. I noticed a year or two ago that when I took the mail around at 10am, everything stopped for 20 minutes. I had an idea and gave it to my boss. She got it cleared by the director and, ever since, we take the mail around just before lunch. Mr Gray, the director, thinks my idea improved productivity and saved time.'

□ *What was the last book you read (or film you saw)? How did it affect you?*

It doesn't really matter what you say about the latest book/film, just as long as you have read/seen it. Don't be like the interviewee who said the name of the first book that came to mind – *In Search of Excellence* – only to be caught by the follow-up: 'To what extent do you agree with Peters' simultaneous loose/tight pronouncements?' Also, by naming such a well-known book, you have managed only to say that you are like millions of others, which doesn't make you stand out in the crowd. Better that you should name something less faddish – that helps to avoid nasty follow-up questions. And you needn't mention the most *recent* book or film you've seen. Your answer must simply make a statement about you as a potential employee. Come up with a response that will set you apart and demonstrate your obvious superiority. Ideally you want to mention a work that in some way has helped you to improve yourself; anything that has honed any of the 20 key personality traits will do.

□ *How do you handle tension?*

This question is different from 'Can you handle pressure?' – it asks *how* you handle it. You could reply, 'Tension is caused when you let things pile up. It is usually caused by letting other areas of responsibility slip by for an extended period. For instance, if you have a difficult presentation coming up, you may procrastinate in your preparations for it. I've seen lots of people do things like that – a task seems so overwhelming they don't know where to begin. I find that if you break those overwhelming tasks into little pieces, they aren't so overwhelming any more. So I suppose I don't so much handle tension as handle the causes of it, by not letting things slip in other areas that can give rise to it.'

☐ *How long have you been looking for another position?*

If you are employed, your answer isn't that important – a short or long time is irrelevant to you in any follow-up probes, because you are just looking for the right job, with the right people and outfit, that offers you the right opportunities. If, on the other hand, you are unemployed at the time of the question, how you answer becomes more important. If you say, 'Well, I've been looking for two years now', it isn't going to score you any points. The interviewer thinks, 'Two years, huh? And no one else wanted him in that time. I wonder what's wrong with him? Well, if no one else is interested, I'm certainly not.' So if you must talk of months or more, be careful to add something like, 'Well, I've been looking for about a year now. I've had a number of offers in that time, but I have decided that, as I spend most of my waking hours at work, the job I take and the people I work with have got to be people with values I can identify with. I made the decision that I wasn't going to suffer clock-watchers and work-to-rule specialists any more.'

☐ *Have you ever been dismissed?*

Say 'no' if you can; if not, act on the advice given to the next question.

☐ *Why were you dismissed?*

If you were made redundant as part of a general workforce reduction, be straightforward and move on to the next topic as quickly as possible. If your employment was terminated with cause, however, this is a very difficult question to answer. Like it or not, termination with cause is usually justified, because the most loathed responsibility of any manager is to take away someone's livelihood. Virtually no one dismisses an employee for kicks.

Looking at that painful event objectively, you will probably find the cause of your dismissal rooted in the absence of one or more of the 20 profiles. The fact that you were dismissed also creates instant doubt in the mind of the interviewer, and greatly increases the chances of your references being checked.

Whatever you do, don't advertise the fact that you were dismissed. If you are asked, be honest, but make sure you package the reason in the best possible light. Perhaps: 'I'm sorry to say, but

I deserved it. I was having some personal problems at the time, and I let them affect my work. I was late to work and lost my motivation. My supervisor – who, by the way, I still speak to – had directions to trim the workforce anyway, and as I'd only been there a couple of years, I was one of the first to go.'

If you can find out the employee turnover figures, voluntary or otherwise, you might add: 'Fifteen other people have left so far this year.' A combination answer of this nature minimises the stigma. You have even managed to demonstrate that you take responsibility for your actions, which shows your analytical and listening skills. If one of your past managers will speak well of you, there is nothing to lose and everything to gain by finishing with: 'Jill Johnson, at the company, would be a good person to check for a reference on what I have told you.'

I would never advise you to be anything but honest in your answers to any interview question. If, however, you have been dismissed by a manager who is still vindictive, take heart: only about 10 per cent of all successful job candidates ever have their references checked.

☐ *Have you ever been asked to resign?*

When someone is asked to resign, it is a gesture on the part of the employer: 'You can resign, or we will dismiss you, so which do you want it to be?' Because you were given the option, though, that employer cannot later say, 'I had to ask him to resign' – that is tantamount to dismissal and could lead to legal problems. In the final analysis, it is safe to answer 'no'.

☐ *In your last job, what were some of the things you spent most of your time on, and why?*

Employees come in two categories: goal-oriented (those who want to get the job done) and task-oriented (those who believe in 'busy' work). You must demonstrate good time management, and that you are, therefore, goal-oriented, for that is what this question probes.

You might reply: 'I work on the telephone like a lot of business-people; meetings also take up a great deal of time. What is more important to me is effective time management. I find more gets achieved in a shorter time if a meeting is scheduled, say, immediately before lunch or at the close of business. I try to allocate my time in the morning and afternoon for major tasks, so I don't get bogged down in 'busy' work. At 4 o'clock, I review what I've achieved, what went right or wrong, and plan adjustments and my main thrust of business for tomorrow.'

☐ *In what ways has your job prepared you to take on greater responsibility?*

This is one of the most important questions you will have to answer. The interviewer is looking for examples of your professional development, perhaps to judge your future growth potential, so you must tell a story that demonstrates it. The following example shows growth, listening skills, honesty and adherence to procedures. Parts of it can be adapted to your personal experience. Notice the then and now aspect of the answer.

'When I first started my last job, my boss would brief me morning and evening. I made some mistakes, learned a lot and got the jobs done on time. As time went by I took on greater responsibilities [list some of them]. Nowadays, we have a meeting every Monday morning to discuss any major directional changes, so that she can keep management informed. I think that demonstrates not only my growth, but also the confidence management has in my judgement and ability to perform consistently above standard.'

☐ *In what ways has your job changed since you originally joined the company?*

You can use the same answer here as for the previous question.

☐ *How does this job compare with others you have applied for?*

This is a variation of more direct questions, such as, 'How many other jobs have you applied for?' and 'Who else have you applied to?' but it is a slightly more intelligent question and therefore more dangerous. It asks you to compare. Answer the question and sidestep at the same time.

'No two jobs are the same, and this one is certainly unlike any other I have applied for.' If you are pressed further, say, 'Well, to give you a more detailed answer, I would need to ask you a number of questions about the job and the company. Would now be a good time to do that or would it be better later in the interview process?'

☐ *What makes this job different from your current/last one?*

If you don't have enough information to answer the question, say so, and ask some questions of your own. Behind the question is the interviewer's desire to uncover experience you are lacking –

your answer could be used as evidence against you. Focus on the positive: 'From what I know of the job, I seem to have all the experience required to make a thorough success. I would say that the major differences seem to be . . .' and here you play back the positive attributes of the department and company as the interviewer gave them to you, either in the course of the interview or in answer to your specific questions.

☐ *Do you have any questions?*

A good question. Almost always, this is a sign that the interview is drawing to a close, and that you have one more chance to make an impression. Remember the old adage: People respect what you inspect, not what you expect. Create questions from any of the following.

- Find out why the job is vacant, who had it last, and what happened to him or her. Was he or she promoted or fired? How many people have held this position in the last couple of years? What happened to them subsequently?
- Why did the interviewer join the company? How long has he or she been there? What is it about the company that keeps him or her there?
- To whom would you report? Will you get the opportunity to meet that person?
- Where is the job located? What are the travel requirements, if any?
- What type of training is required, and how long is it? What type of training is available?
- What would your first assignment be?
- What are the realistic chances for growth in the job? Where are the opportunities for greatest growth within the company?
- What are the skills and attributes most needed to get ahead in the company?
- Who will be the company's major competitors over the next few years? How does the interviewer feel the company stands up against them?
- What has been the growth pattern of the company over the last five years? Is it profitable? How profitable? Is the company privately or publicly owned?
- If there is a written job description, may you see it?
- How regularly do performance appraisals occur? What model do they follow?

Chapter 11

What Kind of Person Are You *Really*, Mr Jones?

Will you reduce your new employer's life expectancy? The interviewer wants to know! If you are offered the job and accept, you will be working together 48 weeks of the year. Every employer wants to know whether you will fit in with the rest of the staff, whether you are a team player and, most of all, whether you are manageable.

There are a number of questions the interviewer might use to probe this area. They will mainly be geared to your behaviour and attitudes in the past. Remember, it is universally believed that your past actions predict your future behaviour.

☐ *How do you take direction?*

This is really two questions. 'How do you take direction?' and 'How do you take criticism?' Your answer will cover both points. 'I take direction well and believe there are two types: carefully explained direction, when my boss has time to treat me with honour and respect; then there is the other – a brusque order or correction. While most people get upset with this, personally I always believe the manager is troubled with bigger problems and a tight schedule. As such I take the direction and get on with the job without taking offence so my boss can get on with her job. It's the only way.'

☐ *Would you like to have your boss's job?*

It is a rare boss who wants his or her livelihood taken. On my very first interview, my future boss said, 'Mr Yate, it has been a pleasure to meet you. However, until you walked in I wasn't looking for a new job. Don't you feel you would be better off with another company?'

By the same token, ambition is admired, but mainly by the ambitious. Be cautiously optimistic. Perhaps: 'Well, if my boss were promoted over the coming years, I hope to have made a strong enough contribution to warrant his recommendation. And I realise there are more skills I have to learn. That's why I'm looking for a fresh opportunity. I'm looking for a manager who will help me to develop my capabilities and grow with him.'

□ *What do you think of your current/last boss?*

Short, sweet and shut up. People who complain about their employers are recognised as the same people who cause the most disruption in the department. Being asked this question means the interviewer has no desire to take on trouble. 'I liked her as a person, respected her professionally and appreciated her guidance.' This question is often followed by one that tries to validate your answer.

□ *Describe a situation where your work or one of your ideas was criticised.*

A doubly dangerous question. You are being asked to say how you handle criticism and to detail your faults. If you are asked this question, describe a poor *idea* that was criticised, *not* poor work. Poor work can cost money and is a warning sign, obviously, to the interviewer.

One of the wonderful things about a new job is that you can leave the past entirely behind, so it does not matter how you handled criticism in the past. What does matter is how the interviewer would *like* you to handle criticism, if and when it becomes his or her unpleasant duty to dish it out; that's what the question is really about. So relate one of those 'it-seemed-like-a-good-idea-at-the-time' anecdotes, and finish with how you handled the criticism. You could say: 'I listened carefully and resisted the temptation to interrupt or defend myself. Then I fed back what I heard to make sure the facts were straight. I asked for advice, we bounced some ideas around, then I came back later and re-presented the idea in a more viable format. My supervisor's input was invaluable.'

□ *Tell me about yourself.*

This is not an invitation to ramble on. You need to know more about the question before giving an answer. 'What area of my background would be most interesting to you?' This will help the interviewer to help you with the appropriate focus, so you can avoid discussing irrelevances. Never answer this question without finding out whether the interviewer wishes to hear about your business or personal life. However the interviewer responds to your qualifying question, the tale you tell should demonstrate one or more of the 20 key personality profiles. Perhaps honesty, integrity, being a team player or determination.

If you choose 'team player', part of your answer might include this: 'I put my heart into everything I do, whether it be sport or work. I find that getting along with your peers and being part of the team makes life more enjoyable and productive.'

□ *Rate yourself on a scale of one to ten.*

A stupid question. That aside, bear in mind that this is meant to plumb the depths of your self-esteem. If you answer ten, you run the risk of portraying yourself as insufferable; on the other hand, if you say less than seven, you might as well get up and leave. You are probably best claiming to be an eight or nine, saying that you always give of your best, but that in doing so you always increase your skills and therefore always see room for improvement.

□ *What kind of things do you worry about?*

Some questions, such as this one, can seem so off-the-wall that you might start treating the interviewer as a father confessor in no time at all. Your private phobias have nothing to do with your job, and revealing them can get you labelled as unbalanced. It is best to confine your answer to the sensible worries of a conscientious professional. 'I worry about deadlines, staff turnover, tardiness, back-up plans for when the computer crashes, or that one of my salespeople burns out or defects to the competition – just the normal stuff. It goes with the territory, so I don't let it get me down.'

□ *What is the most difficult situation you have faced?*

The question looks for information on two fronts: 'How do you define difficult?' and, 'What was your handling of the situation?' You must have a story ready for this one in which the situation was both tough and allowed you to show yourself in a good light. Avoid talking about problems that have to do with co-workers. You can talk about the difficult decision to dismiss someone, but emphasise that once you had examined the problem and reached a conclusion you acted quickly and professionally, with the best interests of the company at heart.

□ *What are some of the things that bother you? What are your pet hates? Tell me about the last time you felt anger on the job.*

These questions are so similar that they can be treated as one. It is tremendously important that you show you can remain calm. Most of us have seen a colleague lose his or her cool on occasion – not a pretty sight and one that every sensible employer wants to avoid. This question comes up more and more often the higher up the corporate ladder you climb and the more frequent your contact with clients and the general public. To answer it, find something that angers conscientious workers. 'I enjoy my work and believe in giving value to my employer. Dealing with clock-watchers and the ones who regularly get sick on Mondays and Fridays really bothers me, but it's not something that gets me angry or anything like that.' An answer of this nature will help you much more than the kind given by a California engineer, who went on for some minutes about how he hated the small mindedness of people who don't like pet rabbits – in the office.

□ *What have you done that shows initiative?*

The question probes whether you are a 'doer', someone who will look for ways to increase sales, save time or save money. The kind of person who gives a manager a pleasant surprise once in a while, who makes life easier for co-workers. Do beware, however, that your example of initiative does not show a disregard for company policies and procedures.

'My boss has to organise a lot of meetings. That means developing agendas, letting employees around the country know the dates well in advance, getting materials printed, etc. Most people in my position sit and wait for the work to be given them. I don't. Every quarter I sit down with my boss and find out the dates of all his meetings for the next six months. I immediately make the hotel and travel arrangements and then work back-wards. I ask myself questions like, "If the agenda for the July meeting is to reach the field at least six weeks beforehand, when must it be finished by?" Then I come up with a deadline. I do this for all the major activities for all the meetings. I put the deadlines in his diary – and mine, only two weeks earlier. That way I remind the boss that the deadline is getting closer. My boss is the best organised, most relaxed manager in the company. None of his colleagues can understand how he does it.'

□ *What are some of the things about which you and your manager disagreed?*

It is safest to state that you did not disagree.

□ *In what areas do you feel your manager could have done a better job?*

The same goes for this one. No one admires the wisdom of hind-sight.

You could reply: 'I have always had the highest respect for my manager. I have always been so busy learning from Mr Jones that

I don't think he could have done a better job. He has really brought me to the point where I am ready for greater challenges. That's why I'm here.'

□ *What are some of the things your manager did that you disliked?*

If you and the interviewer are both non-smokers, for example, and your boss isn't, use it. Apart from that: 'You know, I've never thought of our relationship in terms of like or dislike. I've always thought our role was to get along together and get the work done.'

□ *How well do you feel your boss rated your job performance?*

This is one very sound reason to ask for written evaluations of your work before leaving a company. Some performance review procedures include a written evaluation of your performance – perhaps your company uses it. If you work for a company that asks you to sign your formal review, you are quite entitled to request a copy of it. You should also ask for a letter of recommendation whenever you leave a job: you have nothing to lose. While I don't recommend thrusting recommendations under unwilling interviewer's noses (they smell a rat when written endorsements of any kind are offered unrequested), the time will come when you are asked and can produce them with a flourish. If you don't have written references, perhaps: 'My supervisor always rated my job performance well. In fact, I was always rated as being capable of accepting further responsibilities. The problem was there was nothing available in the company – that's why I'm here.'

If your research has been done properly you can also quote verbal appraisals of your performance from previous jobs. 'In fact, my boss said only a month ago that I was the most valuable [eg] engineer in the workgroup, because . . .'

□ *How did your boss get the best out of you?*

This is a manageability question, geared to probing whether you are going to be a pain in the neck or not. Whatever you say, it is important for your future happiness that you make it clear you don't appreciate being treated like a dishrag. You can give a short, general answer: 'My last boss got superior effort and performance by treating me like a human being and giving me the same personal respect with which she liked to be treated herself.' This book is full of answers that get you out of tight corners and make you shine, but this is one instance in which you really should tell it like it is. You don't want to work for someone who is going to make life miserable for you.

□ *How interested are you in sport?*

A survey of US middle- and upper-management personnel found that the executives who listed group sports/activities among their leisure pursuits made an average of £2,000 per year *more* than their sedentary colleagues. Don't you just love football, suddenly? The interviewer is looking for your involvement in groups as a signal that you know how to get along with others and pull together as a team.

'I really enjoy most team sports. Don't get a lot of time to indulge myself, but I am a regular member of my company's cricket team.' Apart from team sport, endurance sports are seen as a sign of determination: swimming, running and cycling are all acceptable.

□ *What personal characteristics are necessary for success in your field?*

You know the answer to this one: it's a brief recital of key personality profiles.

You might say: 'To be successful in my field? Drive, motivation, energy, confidence, determination, good communication and analytical skills. Combined, of course, with the ability to work with others.'

□ *Do you prefer working with others or alone?*

This question is usually used to determine whether you are a team player. However, before answering be sure you know whether the job *requires* you to work alone. Then answer appropriately. Perhaps: 'I'm quite happy working alone when necessary. I don't need much constant reassurance. But I prefer to work in a group. So much more gets achieved when people pull together.'

□ *Explain your role as a group/team member.*

You are being asked to describe yourself as either a team player or a loner. Most departments depend on harmonious teamwork for their success, so describe yourself as a team player, by all means: 'I perform my job in a way that helps others to do theirs in an efficient fashion. Beyond the mechanics, we all have a responsibility to make the workplace a friendly and pleasant place to be. That means everyone working for the common good and making the necessary personal sacrifices towards that good.'

☐ *How would you define a conducive work atmosphere?*

This is a tricky question, especially because you probably have no idea what kind of work atmosphere exists in that particular office. So the longer your answer, the greater your chances of saying the wrong thing. Keep it short and sweet. 'One where the team has a genuine interest in its work and a desire to turn out a good product/deliver a good service.'

☐ *Do you make your opinions known when you disagree with the views of your manager?*

If you can, state that you come from an environment where input is encouraged when it helps the team's ability to get the job done efficiently. 'If opinions are sought in a meeting, I will give mine, although I am careful to be aware of others' feelings. I will never criticise a co-worker or a superior in open forum; besides, it is quite possible to disagree without being disagreeable. However, my past manager made it clear that she valued my opinion by asking for it. So, after a while, if there was something I felt strongly about, I would make an appointment to sit down and discuss it with her.' You might choose to end by turning the tables with a question of your own: 'Is this a position where we work as a team to solve problems and get the job done, or one where we are meant to be seen and not heard and speak when spoken to?'

☐ *What would you say about a manager who was unfair or difficult to work with?*

For this job, you'll definitely want to meet your potential manager – just in case you have been earmarked for the company Genghis Khan without warning. The response, 'Do you have anyone in particular in mind?' will probably get you off the hook. If you need to elaborate, try: 'I would make an appointment to see the manager and diplomatically explain that I felt uncomfortable in our relationship, that I felt he or she was not treating me as a professional colleague, and therefore that I might not be performing up to standard in some way – that I wanted to right matters and ask for his or her input about what I must do to create a professional relationship. I would enter into the discussion and indicate that we were equally responsible for whatever communication problems existed, and that this wasn't just the manager's problem.'

☐ *Do you consider yourself a natural leader or a born follower?*

How you answer depends a lot on the job offer you are aiming for. If you are a recent graduate, you are expected to have high aspirations, so go for it. If you are already on the corporate ladder with some practical experience in the school of hard knocks, you might want to be a little more cagey. Assuming you are up for and want a leadership position, you might try something like this: 'I would be reluctant to regard anyone as a natural leader. Hiring, motivating and disciplining other adults and at the same time moulding them into a cohesive team involves a number of delicately tuned skills that no honest people can say they were born with. Leadership requires first of all the desire, then it is a lifetime learning process. Anyone who reckons that he or she has it all under control and has nothing more to learn isn't doing the employer any favours.'

Of course, a little humility is also in order, because just about every leader in every company reports to someone, and there is a good chance that you are talking to such a someone right now. So you might consider including something like: 'No matter how well developed any individual's leadership qualities, an integral part of the skills of a leader is to take direction from his or her immediate boss, and also to seek the input of the people being supervised. The wise leader will always follow good advice and sound business judgement wherever it comes from. I would say that, given the desire to be a leader, the true leader in the modern business world must embrace both.' How can anyone disagree with that kind of wisdom?

☐ *Why do you feel you are a better [eg] secretary than some of your co-workers?*

If you speak disparagingly of your co-workers, you will not put yourself in the best light. That is what the question asks you to do, so it poses some difficulties. The trick is to answer the question but not to accept the invitation to show yourself from anything other than a flattering perspective. 'I think that question is best answered by a manager. It is so difficult to be objective, and I really don't like to slight my co-workers. I don't spend my time thinking about how superior I am, because that would be detrimental to our working together as a team. I believe, however, some of the qualities that make me an outstanding secretary are . . .' and you go on to illustrate job-related personal qualities that make you a beacon of productivity and a joy to work with.

☐ *You have a doctor's appointment arranged for noon. You've waited two weeks. An urgent meeting is scheduled at the last moment, though. What do you do?*

What a crazy question, you mutter. It's not. It is even more than a question – it is what I call a question shell. The question within the shell – in this instance, 'Will you sacrifice the appointment or sacrifice your job?' – can be changed at will. This is a situational-interviewing technique, which poses an on-the-job problem to see how the prospective employee will respond. A Chicago company asks this question as part of its initial screening and, if you give the wrong answer, you never even get a face-to-face interview. So what is the right answer to this or any similar shell question?

Fortunately, once you understand the interviewing technique, it is quite easy to handle – all you have to do is turn the question around. 'If I were the manager who had to schedule a really important meeting at the last moment, and someone on my staff chose to go to the doctor's instead, how would I feel?'

It is unlikely that you would be an understanding manager unless the visit were for a triple bypass. To answer, you start with an evaluation of the importance of the problem and the responsibility of everyone to make some sacrifices for the organisation, and finish with: 'The first thing I would do is reschedule the appointment and save the doctor's office incon-venience. Then I would immediately make sure that I was properly prepared for the emergency meeting.'

☐ *How do you manage to attend an interview while still employed?*

As long as you don't explain that you invented a dental appointment in order to go to the interview you should be all right. Beware of revealing anything that might make you appear at all underhand. Best to make the answer short and sweet and let the interviewer move on to richer areas of inquiry. Just explain that you had some holiday due, or took a day off in lieu of overtime. 'I had some holiday to take, so I went to my boss and explained that I needed a couple of days off for some personal business, and asked her what days would be most suitable. Although I plan to change jobs, I don't in any way want to hurt my current employer in the process by being absent during a crisis.'

☐ *When do you expect a promotion?*

Tread warily, show you believe in yourself and have both feet firmly planted on the ground. 'That depends on a few things. Of course, I cannot expect promotion without the performance that marks me as deserving promotion. I also need to join a company that has the growth necessary to provide the opportunity. I hope that my manager believes in promoting from within and will help me to grow so that I will have the skills necessary to be considered for promotion when the opportunity comes along.'

If you are the only one doing a particular job in the company, or you are in management, you need to build another factor into your answer. For example: 'As a manager, I realise that part of my job is to have done my succession planning, and that I must have someone trained and ready to step into my shoes before I can expect to step up. That way I play my part in preserving the chain of command.' To avoid being caught off guard with queries about your having achieved that in your present job, you can finish with: 'Just as I have done in my present job, where I have a couple of people capable of taking over the reins when I leave.'

□ *Tell me a story.*

What on earth does the interviewer mean by that question? You don't know until you get him or her to elaborate. Ask, 'What would you like me to tell you a story about?' Any other response is to risk making a fool of yourself. Very often the question is asked to see how analytical you are: people who answer the question without finding out more show that they do not think things through carefully. The subsequent question will be about either your personal or professional life. If it is about your personal life, tell a story that shows you like people and are determined. Do *not* discuss your love life. If the subsequent question is about your professional life, tell a story that demonstrates your willingness and manageability.

□ *What have your other jobs taught you?*

By all means, talk about the skills you have learned. Many interviewees have had success finishing their answer with: 'There are two general things I have learned from past jobs. The first is: if you are confused, ask. It's better to ask a naïve question than make a stupid mistake. The second is: it is better to promise less and produce more.'

□ *Define cooperation.*

The question asks you to explain how to function as a team

player in the workplace. Your answer could be: 'Cooperation is a person's ability to sacrifice personal wishes and beliefs whenever necessary to ensure the department reaches its goals. It is also a person's desire to be part of a team, and by hard work and goodwill make the department greater than the sum of its parts.'

☐ *What difficulties do you have tolerating people with different backgrounds and interests from yours?*

Another 'team player' question with the awkward inference that you *do* have problems. Give the following answer: 'I don't have *any.*'

☐ *With hindsight, what have you done that was a little harebrained?*

You are never harebrained in your business dealings, and you haven't been harebrained in your personal life since graduation, right? The only safe examples to use are ones from your deep past that ultimately turned out well. One of the best to use, if it applies to you, is this one: 'Well, I guess the time I bought my house. I had no idea what I was letting myself in for and, at the time, I really couldn't afford it. Still, I managed to make the payments, though I had to work like someone possessed. Yes, my first house – that was a real learning experience.' Not only can most people relate to this example, but it also gives you the opportunity to sell one or two of your very positive and endearing traits.

Now if you think the interview is only tough for the interviewee, it's time to take a look at the other side of the desk.

Chapter 12
The Other Side of the Desk

There are two terrible places to be during an interview: sitting in front of the desk wondering what on earth is going to happen next, and sitting behind the desk asking the questions. The average interviewer dreads the meeting almost as much as the interviewee, yet for opposite reasons.

Business frequently yields to the mistaken belief that any person, on being promoted into the ranks of management, becomes mystically endowed with all the necessary managerial skills. This is a fallacy. Comparatively few management people have been taught to interview; most just bumble along and pick up a certain proficiency over a period of time.

There are two distinct types of interviewer who can spell disaster for you if you are unprepared. One is the highly skilled interviewer who has been trained in systematic techniques for probing your past for all the facts and evaluating your potential. The other is the totally incompetent interviewer who may even lack the ability to phrase a question adequately.

The skilful interview

Skilful interviewers know exactly what they want to discover. They have taken exhaustive steps to learn the strategies that will help them to appoint only the best for their company. They follow a set format for the interview process to ensure objectivity in selection and a set sequence of questions to ensure the facts are gathered. This type of interviewer will definitely test your mettle.

There are many ways for a manager to build and conduct a structured interview, but all have the same goals:

- To ensure a systematic coverage of your work history and applicable job-related skills
- To provide a technique for gathering all the relevant facts

- To provide a uniform strategy that objectively evaluates all job candidates.
- To determine ability, willingness and manageability.

Someone using structured interview techniques will usually follow a standard format. The interview will begin with a small talk and a brief introduction to relax you. Following close on the heels of this chit-chat comes a statement geared to assure you that baring your faults is the best way to get the job. Your interviewer will then outline the steps in the interview. This will include your giving a chronological description of your work history, and then the interviewer asking some questions about your experience. Then, before the close of the interview, you will be given an opportunity to ask your own questions.

Sounds pretty simple, huh? Well, watch out! The skilled interviewer knows exactly what questions will be asked, why, in what order and what the desired responses are. Every applicant for the job will be interviewed and evaluated in exactly the same fashion. You are up against a pro.

Like the hunter who learns to think like his prey, the best way to win over this interviewer is to *think* like the interviewer. In fact, take the process a little further in subtlety: you must win, but you don't want the others to realise you beat them at their own game. To do this, you must learn how the interviewer has prepared for you; and by going through the same process you will beat your competitors for the job offer.

The dangerous part of this type of interview is called 'skills evaluation'. The interviewer has analysed all the different skills it takes to do the job, and all the personality traits that complement those skills. Armed with this data, he or she has developed a series of carefully sequenced questions to draw out your relative merits and weaknesses.

Graphically, it looks like the diagram opposite. Letters A–F are the separate skills necessary to do the job; numbers 1–20 are questions asked to identify and verify that particular skill.

This is where many of the tough questions will arise. The only way to prepare effectively is to take the interviewer's viewpoint and complete this exercise in its entirety:

- Look at the position you seek. What role does it play in helping the company to achieve its corporate mission and make a profit?
- What are the five most important duties of that job?

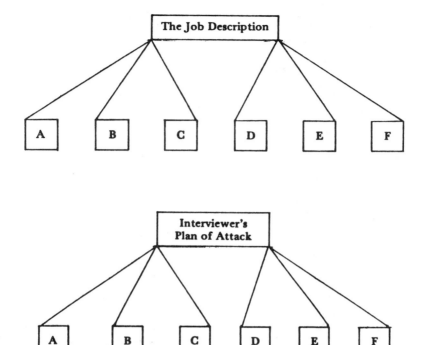

- From a management viewpoint, what are the skills and attributes necessary to perform each of these tasks?

Write all this down. This exercise requires a degree of objectivity, but it will generate multiple job offers.

Now put yourself in the interviewer's shoes. What topics would you examine to find out whether a person can really do the job? If for some reason you get stuck with this process, just use your past experience. You have worked with good and bad people. Their work habits and skills will lead you to develop both the potential questions and the correct answers.

Each job skill you identify is fertile ground for the interviewer's questions. Don't forget the intangible skills that are so important to many jobs, like self-confidence or creativity, because the interviewer won't. Develop a number of questions for each job skill you identify.

Again, looking back at co-workers (and still wearing the manager's mask), what are the personal characteristics that would make life comfortable or uncomfortable for you as a manager? These are also dimensions that are likely to be probed by the interviewer. Once you have identified the questions you would ask in the manager's position, the answers should come easily.

This is the way managers are trained to develop structured interview questions; I just gave you the inside track. Complete the exercise by developing the answers you would like to hear as a manager. Take time to complete the exercise conscientiously, writing out both the questions and appropriate answers.

The professional interviewer

These sharks have some juicy questions to probe your skills, attitude and personality. Would you like to hear some of them? Notice that all the questions in this section lay out a problem, but in no way lead you to the answer. They are all two-part questions, and some are three. The additional question that can be tagged on to them *all* is, 'What did you learn from this experience?' Assume this is included whenever you get one of these questions; you'll be able to sell different aspects of your success profile.

☐ *You have been given a project that requires you to interact with different levels within the company. How do you do this? What levels are you most comfortable with?*

This is a two-part question that probes your self-confidence and your communication skills. The first part asks how you interact with superiors and how you motivate those working for you on the project. The second part of the question is saying, 'Tell me who you regard as your peer group; help me to pigeonhole and categorise you.' To cover these bases you will want to include the essence of this: 'There are basically two types of people I would interact with on a project of this nature. Those I report to, who bear ultimate responsibility for its success. With them I determine deadlines and how they will evaluate the success of the project. I outline my approach, breaking the project down into component parts, getting approval on both the approach and costs. I would keep my supervisors up to date on a regular basis, and seek input whenever needed. My supervisors would expect three things from me: the facts, an analysis of potential problems, and that I not be intimidated, as this could jeopardise the project's success. I would comfortably satisfy all these expectations.

'The other people to interact with in a project like this are those who work with me and for me. With these people I would outline the project and explain how successful completion will benefit the company. I would assign the component parts to those best suited to each, arrange follow-up times to ensure completion by deadline. My role here would be to direct, motivate and bring the different personalities together to form a team.

'As to comfort level, I find this type of approach enables me to interact comfortably with all levels and types of people.'

☐ *Tell me about an event that really challenged you. How did you meet the challenge? In what way was your approach different from the others?*

This is a straightforward two-part question. The first part probes your problem-solving abilities. The second asks you to set yourself apart from the herd. First of all, outline the problem. The blacker you make the situation look, the better. Having done this, go ahead and explain your solution, its value to your employer and how it was different from other approaches.

'My company is a sales organisation; I was responsible for 70 sales offices across the country. My job was to visit each office once a year, build market strategies with management, and train and motivate the sales force. Then the recession hit. The need to service the sales force was still there, but we couldn't justify the travel cost.

'Morale was an especially important factor; you can't let the sales force feel defeated. I reapportioned my reduced budget and did the following: I dramatically increased my telephone contact with the offices. I instituted a monthly sales technique letter – how to prospect for new clients, how to negotiate difficult sales, etc. I bought and rented sales training and motivational tapes and sent them to my managers with instructions on how to use them in a sales meeting. I stopped visiting all the offices. Instead, I scheduled weekend training meetings in central locations throughout my area: one day of sales training and one day of management training – how to run sales meetings, early termination of low producers, etc.

'While my colleagues complained about the drop in sales, mine increased, albeit a modest 6 per cent. After six months my approach was officially adopted by the company.'

☐ *Give me an example of a method of working you have used. How did you feel about it?*

You have a choice of giving an example of either good or bad work habits. Give a good example, one that demonstrates your understanding of corporate goals, your organisational skills, analytical ability or time management skills.

You could say: 'I believe in giving an honest day's work for a day's pay. That requires organisation and time management. I do my paperwork at the end of each day, when I review the day's achievements; with this done, I plan for tomorrow. When I come to work in the morning, I'm ready to get going without wasting time. I try to schedule meetings shortly before lunch; people get to the point more quickly if it's in their own time. I feel this is a most efficient and organised method of working.'

☐ *When you joined your last company and met the group for the first time, how did you feel? How did you get on with them?*

Your answer should include, 'I naturally felt a little nervous, but I was excited about the new job. I shared that excitement with my new friends, told them that I was enthusiastic about learning new skills from them. I was open and friendly and, when given the opportunity to help someone myself, I jumped at it.'

☐ *In your last job, how did you plan to interview?*

That's an easy one. Just give a description of how the skilled interviewer prepares.

☐ *How have you benefited from your disappointments?*

Disappointments are different from failures. It is an intelligent – probably trained – interviewer who asks this one; it is also an opportunity for the astute interviewee to shine. The question itself is very positive – it asks you to show how you benefited. Note also that it doesn't ask you to give specific details of specific disappointments, so you don't have to open your mouth and put your foot in it. Instead, be general. Edison once explained his success as an inventor by claiming that he knew more ways not to do something than anyone else living; you could do worse than quote him. In any event, sum up your answer with, 'I treat disappointment as a learning experience; I look at what happened, why it happened and how I would do things differently at each stage should the same set of circumstances appear again. That way, I put disappointment behind me and am ready with renewed vigour and understanding to face the new day's problems.'

A side note. A person with strong religious beliefs may be tempted to answer a question like this in terms of religious values. If you benefit from disappointments in a spiritual way, remember that not everyone feels the same as you. And making an interviewer feel awkward is not the way to win the job offer.

□ *What would you do when you had a decision to make and no procedure existed?*

This question probes your analytical skills, integrity and dedication. Most of all, the interviewer is testing your reaction to the 'company way of doing things'. You need to cover that with: 'I would only act without my supervisor's direction if the situation was urgent and the supervisor was not available. Then I would take command of the situation, make a decision and implement it. I would update my boss at the earliest opportunity.' If possible, tell a story to illustrate your approach.

□ *That is an excellent answer. Now to give me a balanced view, can you give me an example that didn't work out so well?*

There are two techniques that every skilled interviewer will use, especially if you are giving good answers. In this question, the interviewer looks for negative balance; in the follow-up, the person will look for negative confirmation. Here, you are required to give an example of an inadequacy. The trick is to pull something from the past, not the present, and to finish with what you learned from the experience. For example: 'That's easy. When I first joined the workforce, I didn't really understand the importance of systems and procedures. There was one time when I was too anxious to contribute and didn't have the full picture. There was a sales visit report everyone had to fill out after visiting a customer. I always put a lot of effort into it until I realised it was never read; it just went in the files. So I stopped doing it for a few days to see if it made any difference. I thought I was gaining time to make more sales for the company. I was so proud of my extra sales calls I told the boss at the end of the week. My boss explained that the records were for the long term, so that should my job change, the next salesperson would have the benefit of a full client history. It was a long time ago, but I have never forgotten the lesson – there's always a reason for systems and procedures. I've had the best kept records in the company ever since.'

To look for negative confirmation, the interviewer may then say something like, 'Thank you. Now can you give me another example?' He or she is trying to confirm a weakness. If you help, you could well do yourself out of a job. Here's your reaction. You sit deep in thought for a good ten seconds, then look up and say firmly, 'No, that's the only occasion when anything like that happened.' Shut up and refuse to be enticed further.

The incompetent interviewer

Now you should be ready for almost anything a professional interviewer could throw at you. Your foresight and strategic planning will generate multiple offers of employment for you in all circumstances except one, and that's when you face the unconsciously incompetent interviewer. This one circumstance is probably more dangerous to your job-offer status than everything else combined.

This problem is embodied in the experienced manager who is a poor interviewer, but does not know it. This person, consciously or otherwise, bases recruiting decisions on 'experience', 'knowledge of mankind' and 'gut feeling'. He or she is an unconscious incompetent. You have probably been interviewed by one in your time. Remember leaving an interview and, upon reflection, feeling the interviewer knew absolutely nothing about you or your skills? If so, you know how frustrating that can be. Here, you'll see how to turn this difficult situation to your advantage. In the future, good managers who are poor interviewers will be offering you jobs with far greater frequency than ever before. Understand that a poor interviewer can be a wonderful manager; interviewing skills are learned, not inherited or created as a result of a mystical corporate blessing.

The unconscious incompetents abound. Their heinous crime can only be exceeded by your inability *to recognise and take advantage of* the proffered opportunity.

As in handling the skilled interviewer, it is necessary to imagine how the unconscious incompetent thinks and feels.

There are many manifestations of the poor interviewer. After each example, follow instructions for appropriate handling of the unique problems each type poses for you.

Example 1. The interviewer's desk is cluttered, and the CV or application that was handed to him or her a few minutes before cannot be found.

Response. Sit quietly through the bumbling and search. Check the surroundings. Breathe deeply and slowly to calm any natural interview nerves. As you bring your adrenalin under control, you do the same thing to the interviewer and the interview. This first example is usually the most common sign of the unconscious incompetent.

Example 2. The interviewer experiences constant interruptions from the telephone or people walking into the office.
Response. This provides good opportunities for selling yourself. Make a note on your pad of where you were in the conversation and refresh the interviewer on the point when you start talking again. He or she will be impressed with your level head and good memory. These interruptions also give time, perhaps, to find something of common interest in the office, something you can compliment. You will also have time to compose the suitable value key follow-up to the point made in the conversation before the interruption.

Example 3. This is the interviewer who starts with an explanation of why you are both sitting there, and then allows the conversation to degenerate into a lengthy diatribe about the company.
Response. Show interest in the company and the conversation. Sit straight, look attentive (the other applicants probably fall asleep), make appreciative murmurs and nod at the appropriate times until there is a pause. When this occurs, comment that this background on the company is much appreciated, because you can now see more clearly how the job fits into the general scheme of things; that you see, for example, how valuable communication skills would be for the job. Could the interviewer please tell you some of the other job requirements? Then, as the job's functions are described, you can interject appropriate information about your background with: 'Would it be of value, Mr Smith, if I described my experience with...?'

Example 4. In this example, the interviewer begins with, or quickly breaks into, the drawbacks of the job. The job may even be described in totally negative terms. This is often done without giving a balanced view of the duties and expectations of the position.
Response. An initial negative description invariably means the interviewer has had bad experiences with staff for this position. Your course is to *empathise* (not sympathise) with his bad

experiences and make it known that you recognise the importance of (for example) *reliability*, especially in this particular type of job. (You will invariably find in these instances that what your interviewer has lacked in the past is someone with a serious understanding of value keys.) Illustrate your proficiency in this particular aspect of your profession with a short example from your work history. Finish your statements by asking the company representative what are some of the biggest problems to be handled in this job. The questions demonstrate your understanding, and the interviewer's answers outline the areas from your background and skills to which you should draw attention.

Example 5. The interviewer will spend considerable time early in the interview describing 'the type of people we *are* here at Company Limited'.
Response. Very simple. You have always wanted to work for a company with this atmosphere. It creates the type of work environment that is conducive to a person really giving his or her best efforts.

Example 6. The interviewer will ask you closed-ended questions. These questions demand no more than a yes/no answer (eg 'Do you pay attention to detail?'). These questions are hardly adequate to establish your skills, yet you must handle them effectively to secure the job offer.
Response. A yes/no answer to a closed-ended question will not get you that offer. The trick is to treat each closed-ended question as if the company representative has added, 'Please give me a brief yet thorough answer.' Closed-ended questions are often mingled with statements followed by pauses. In this instance, agree with the statement in a way that demonstrates both a grasp of your job and the interviewer's statement. For example; 'That's an excellent point, Mr Smith, I couldn't agree more that the attention to detail you describe naturally affects cost containment. My track record in this area...'

Example 7. The interviewer asks a continuing stream of negative questions (as described in Chapter 13).
Response. Use the techniques and answers described earlier. Give your answers with a smile and do not take these questions as personal insults; they are not intended that way. The more stressful the situations the job is likely to place you in, the greater

the likelihood of having to field negative questions. The interviewer wants to know if you can take the heat.

Example 8. The interviewer has difficulty looking at you while speaking.
Response. The interviewer is someone who finds it uncomfortable being in the spotlight. Try to help him or her to be a good audience. Ask specific questions about the job responsibilities and offer your skills in turn: 'Would it be of value to you if I described...'

Multiple interviewers

Often an interviewing manager will arrange for you to meet two or three other people. Frequently, these other interviewers have neither been trained in the appropriate interviewing skills nor told the details of the job for which you are being interviewed. So take additional copies of your executive briefing with you to the interview to help these additional interviewers to focus on the appropriate job functions.

When you understand how to recognise and respond to these different types of interviewer, you will leave your interview having made a favourable first impression. No one forgets first impressions.

Chapter 13

The Stress Interview

To all intents and purposes, every interview is a stress interview, and is stressful by its very nature: the interviewer's questions can act merely as the catalyst for your own fear. The only way to combat this fear is to be prepared, to know what the interviewer is trying to do, to anticipate the various tacks he or she will take. Indeed, that is why you are reading *Great Answers* in the first place, because preparedness is what will keep you cool and collected. Whenever you are ill-prepared for an interview, no one will be able to put more pressure on you than yourself.

This chapter is about the narrower definition of the stress interview, but everything you have already learned in this book applies, and all the techniques you now understand will see you through. Remember: a 'stress' interview is just a regular interview with the volume turned up; the music's the same, just louder.

You've heard the horror stories. An interviewer demands, 'Sell me this pen,' or asks, 'How would you improve the design of a teddy bear?' Or you are faced with a battery of interviewers, all rapid-firing questions like, 'You're giving a dinner party. Which ten famous people would you invite and why?' and one interviewer asks, 'Living or dead?' while another sneers, 'Ten of each.'

Such awful-sounding questions are thrown in to test your poise, to see how you react under pressure and to plumb the depths of your confidence. Many people ruin their chances by reacting to them as personal insults rather than the challenge and opportunity to shine that they really represent.

Previously restricted to the executive suite for the selection of high-powered executives, stress interviews are now established throughout the professional world. And they can come complete with all the intimidating and treacherous tricks your worst dreams can devise. Yet your good performance at a stress interview can mean the difference between life in the corporate fast lane and a stalled career. The questioners in a stress interview are experienced and well organised, with tightly structured procedures and advanced interviewing techniques. The questions and tension they generate have the cumulative effect of throwing you off-balance and revealing the 'real' you rather than someone who can respond with last night's rehearsed answers to six or seven stock questions.

Stress questions can be turned to your advantage or merely avoided by nifty footwork. Whichever way you cope, you will be among a select few who understand this line of questioning. As always, remember with the questions in this chapter to build a personalised answer that reflects your experience and profession. Practise them aloud – by doing that, your responses to these interview gambits will become part of you, and that enhancement of your mental attitude will affect your confidence positively during an interview. You might even consider making a tape of tough questions, spacing them at intervals of 30 seconds to two minutes. You can then play the tape back and answer the questions.

As we will see in this chapter, reflexive questions can prove especially useful when the heat is on. Stress questions are designed to sort out the best team players from those who slow down under pressure. Used with discretion, the reflexives ('. . . don't you think?') will demonstrate to the interviewer that you are able to function well under pressure. At the same time, of course, you put the ball back in the interviewer's court.

One stress interview technique is to set you up for a fall: a pleasant conversation, one or a series of seemingly innocuous questions to relax your guard, then a dazzling series of jabs and body-blows that leave you gibbering. For instance, an interviewer might lull you into a false sense of security by asking some relatively stressless questions: 'What was your initial starting salary at your last job?' then, 'What is your salary now?' then, 'Do you receive bonuses?' etc. To put you on the ropes, he or she then completely surprises you with 'Tell me what sort of troubles you have living within your means.' Such interviewers are using stress in an intelligent fashion, to simulate the unexpected and sometimes tense events of everyday business life. Seeing how you handle simulated pressure gives a fair indication of how you will react to the real thing.

The sophisticated interviewer talks very little, perhaps only 20 per cent of the time, and that time is spent asking questions. Few comments, and no editorialising on your answers, means that you get no hint, verbal or otherwise, about your performance.

The questions are planned, targeted, sequenced and layered. The interviewer covers one subject thoroughly before moving on. Let's take the simple example of 'Can you work under pressure?' As a reader of *Great Answers*, you will know to answer this question with an example, and thereby deflect the main thrust of the stress technique. The interviewer will be prepared for a simple yes/no answer, and what follows is how he or she will keep the unprepared reeling.

☐ *Can you work under pressure?*

A simple, closed-ended question that requires just a yes/no answer, but you don't get off so easily.

☐ *Good, I'd be interested to hear about a time when you experienced pressure on your job.*

An open-ended request to tell a story about a pressure situation. After this, you will be subjected to the layering technique, six layers in the following instance. Imagine how tangled you could get without preparation.

☐ *Why do you think this situation arose?*

☐ *When exactly did this happen?*

(Watch out! Your story of saving hundreds from the burning building may well be checked with your references.)

☐ *What in hindsight were you most dissatisfied with about your performance?*

Here we go. You're trying to show how well you perform under pressure, then suddenly you're telling tales against yourself.

☐ *How do you feel others involved could have acted more responsibly?*

An open invitation to criticise peers and superiors, which you should diplomatically decline.

☐ *Who holds the responsibility for this occurrence?*

Another invitation to point the finger of blame.

☐ *Where in the chain of command can steps be taken to avoid this sort of thing happening again?*

You have just been through an old reporter's technique of asking why, when, who, what, how and where. This technique can be applied to any question you are asked and is frequently used to probe those success stories that sound just too good to be true.

You'll find them suddenly tagged on to the simple closed-ended questions as well as to the open-ended ones, starting, 'Share with me ...,' 'Tell me about a time when ...,' or, 'I'm interested in finding out about ...,' and requesting specific examples from your work history.

After you've survived this barrage, a friendly tone will conceal another zinger: 'What did you learn from the experience?' It's a question that is geared to probing your judgement and emotional maturity. Your answer will be to emphasise whichever of the key personality traits your story was illustrating.

When the interviewer feels you are on the edge of revealing something unusual in an answer, 'mirror statements' will be employed. The last key phrase of your answer will be repeated or paraphrased, and followed by a steady gaze and silence: 'So, you learned that organisation is the key to management.' The idea is that the quiet remark and expectant look will work together to make you continue talking. It can give you a most disconcerting feeling to find yourself rambling on without quite knowing why. The trick to this is knowing when to stop. When the interviewer gives you the expectant look, expand your answer (you have to), but by no more than a couple of sentences. Otherwise, you will get that creepy feeling that you're digging yourself another hole.

There will be times when you face more than one interviewer at a time. When it happens, remember the story of one woman who had five interviewers all asking questions at the same time. As the poor interviewee got halfway through one answer, another question would be shot at her. Pausing for breath, she smiled and said, 'Hold your horses. These are all excellent questions, and given time, I'll answer them all. Now who's next?' In so doing, she showed the interviewers exactly what they wanted to see and what, incidentally, is behind every stress interview; the search for poise and calm under fire, combined with a refusal to be intimidated.

You never know when a stress interview will raise its ugly head. Often it can be that rubber-stamp meeting with the senior executive at the end of a series of gruelling meetings. This is not always surprising: while other interviewers are concerned with determining whether you are able, willing and manageable for the job in question, the senior executive who eventually throws you off balance is the one who is probing you for potential promotability.

The most intimidating stress interviews are recognisable

before the interviewer speaks: no eye contact, no greeting, either silence or a non-committal grunt, no small talk and a general air of boredom, lack of interest or thinly veiled aggression. The first words you hear could well be 'Go ahead, then, I don't have all day.' In these situations, forewarned is forearmed, so here are some of the questions you can expect to follow such openings.

☐ *What is your greatest weakness?*

This is a direct invitation to put your heard in a noose. Decline the invitation.

If there is a minor part of the job where you lack knowledge – but knowledge that you will obviously pick up quickly – use that. For instance: 'I haven't worked with this type of spreadsheet program before but, given my experience with six other types, I don't think it should take me more than a couple of days to pick it up.' Here you remove the emphasis from weakness and put it on to a developmental problem that is easily overcome. Be careful, though – this very effective ploy must be used with discretion.

Another good option is to give a generalised answer that takes advantage of value keys. Design the answer so that your weakness is ultimately a positive characteristic. For example: 'I enjoy my work and always give each project my best shot. So when sometimes I don't feel that others are pulling their weight, I find it a little frustrating. I am aware of that weakness, and in those situations I try to overcome it with a positive attitude that I hope will catch on.'

Also consider the technique of putting it in the past. Here you take a weakness from the distant past, and show how you overcame it. It answers the question but ends on a positive note. Here is an illustration: 'When I first got into this field, I always had problems with my paperwork – you know, keeping adequate records. And to be honest, I let them slip once or twice. My manager sat me down and explained the potential troubles such behaviour could cause. I really took it to heart, and I think you will find my record-keeping system is one of the best around today. You only have to tell me something once.' With that kind of answer, you also get the added bonus of showing that you accept and act on criticism.

Congratulations! You have just turned a bear of a question into an opportunity to sell yourself with your professional profile. In deciding on the particular answer you will give, remember that the interviewer isn't really concerned about your general weaknesses – none of us is a saint outside the interview room. He or she is simply concerned about any red flags that might signal your inability to perform the job or be manageable in the performance of your duties.

□ *With hindsight, how could you have improved your progress?*

Here's a question that demands, 'Tell me your mistakes and weaknesses.' If you can mention ways of improving your performance without damaging your candidacy, do so. The end of your answer should contain something like: 'Other than that, I don't know what to add. I have always done my best.' Then shut up.

□ *What kind of decisions are most difficult for you?*

You are human, admit it, but be careful what you admit. If you have ever had to dismiss someone, you are in luck, because no one likes to do that. Emphasise that having reached a logical conclusion, you act. If you are not in management, tie your answer to key profiles: 'It's not that I have difficulty making decisions – some just require more consideration than others. A small example might be holiday time. Now, everyone is entitled to it, but I don't believe you should leave your boss in the lurch at short notice. I think very carefully at the beginning of the year when I'd like to take my holiday, and then think of alternative dates. I go to my manager, tell him what I hope to do, and see whether there is any conflict. I wouldn't want to be out of the office for the two weeks before a project deadline, for instance. So by carefully considering things far enough in advance, I don't procrastinate, and I make sure my plans fit in with my boss and the department for the year.'

Here you take a trick question and use it to demonstrate your consideration, analytical abilities and concern for the department – and for the company bottom line.

□ *Tell me about the problems you have living within your means.*

This is a twister to catch you off-guard. Your best defence is first of all to know that it exists, and, second, to give it short shrift. 'I know few people who are satisfied with their current earnings. As a professional, I am continually striving to improve my skills and to improve my standard of living. But my problems are no different from that of this company or any other – making sure that all the bills are paid on time and recognising that every month and year there are some things that must be taken care of and other expenses that are best deferred.'

☐ *What area of your skills/professional development do you want to improve at this time?*

Another tell-me-all-your-weaknesses question. You should try to avoid damaging your candidacy by tossing around careless admissions. One effective answer is to say, 'Well, from what you have told me about the job, I seem to have all the necessary skills and background. What I would really find exciting is the opportunity to work on a job where . . .' At this point, you replay the interviewer's hot buttons about the job. You emphasise that you really have all the job-related skills and also tell the interviewer what you find exciting about the job. It works admirably.

Another safe response is to reiterate one or two areas that combine personal strengths and the job's most crucial responsibilities, and finish with saying, 'These areas are so important that I don't think anyone can be too good or should ever stop trying to polish skills.'

☐ *Your application shows you have been with one company a long time without any appreciable increase in rank or salary. Tell me about this.*

This is a tough one. To start with, you should analyse why this state of affairs exists (assuming the interviewer's assessment is accurate). Then, when you have determined the cause, practise saying it out loud to yourself as you would say it during an actual interview. It may take a few tries. Chances are that no matter how valid your explanation really is, it will come off sounding a little tinny or vindictive without some polishing. Avoid the sour grapes syndrome at all costs.

Here are some tactics you can use. First of all, try to avoid putting your salary history on application forms. No one is going to deny you an interview for lack of salary history if your skills match those which the job requires. Of course, you should never put such trivia on your CV.

If the interviewer is intent, and asks you outright for this information, you'll find a great response on page 155, in the chapter on salary negotiations.

Now then. We address next the delicate matter of 'hey-wait-a-minute-why-no-promotions?' This is one case where saying the wrong thing can get you in just as much trouble as failing to say the right thing. The interviewer has posed a truly negative inquiry; the more time either of you spend on it, the more time the interviewer has to devote to concentrating on negative aspects of your candidacy. Make your answer short and sweet, then shut up. For instance, 'My current employer is a stable company with a good working environment, but there's minimal growth there in my area – in fact, there hasn't been any promotion in my area since _____ Your question is the reason I am meeting here with you; I have the skills and ability to take on more responsibility and I'm looking for a place to do that.'

☐ *Are you willing to take calculated risks when necessary?*

First, qualify the question: 'How do you define calculated risks? What sort of risks? Give me an example of a risk you have in mind; what are the stakes involved?' That will show you exactly the right analytical approach to evaluating a calculated risk and, while the interviewer is rattling on, you have bought time to come up with an answer. Whatever your answer, you will include, 'Naturally, I would never take any risk that would in any way jeopardise the safety or reputation of my company or colleagues. In fact, I don't think any employer would appreciate an employee at any level taking risks of any nature without first having a thorough briefing and exchanging ideas.'

☐ *See this pen I'm holding? Sell it to me.*

Not a request, as you might think, that would be asked only of a salesperson. In today's business world, everyone is required to sell – sometimes products, but more often ideas, approaches and concepts. As such, you are being tested to see whether you understand the basic concepts of features-and-benefits selling, how quickly you think on your feet and how effective your verbal communication is. For example, the interviewer holds up a broad-tip yellow highlighter. You say calmly, 'Let me tell you about the special features of this product. First of all, it's a highlighter that will emphasise important points in reports or articles, and that will save you time in recalling the important features. The casing is wide enough to enable you to use it comfortably at your desk or on a flip chart. It has a flat base you can stand it up on. Costing under a pound, it is disposable – and affordable enough for you to have a handful for your desk, briefcase, car and at home. And the bright yellow colour means you'll never lose it.'

Then close with a smile and a question of your own that will bring a smile to your interviewer's face: 'How many gross shall we deliver?'

□ *How will you be able to cope with a change in environment after [eg] five years with your current company?*

Another chance to take an implied negative and turn it into a positive. 'That's one of the reasons I want to make a change. After five years with my current employer, I felt I was about to get stale. Everyone needs a change of scene once in a while. It's just time for me to make some new friends, face some new challenges and experience some new approaches; I hope I'll have the chance to contribute from my experience.'

□ *Why aren't you earning more at your age?*

Accept this as a compliment to your skills and accomplishments. 'I have always felt that solid experience would stand me in good stead in the long run and that earnings would come in due course. Also, I am not the type of person to change jobs just for the money. At this point, I have a solid background that is worth something to a company.' Now, to avoid the interviewer putting you on the spot again, finish with a question: 'How much should I be earning now?' The figure could be your offer.

□ *What is the worst thing you have heard about our company?*

If you have heard anything truly bad about the outfit, you shouldn't be there in the first place, so it is safe to assume you haven't. Nevertheless, the question can come as something of a shock. As with all stress questions, your poise under stress is vital. If you can carry off a halfway decent answer as well, you are a winner. The best response to this question is simple. Just say with a smile: 'You're a tough company to get into because your interviews are so rigorous.' It's true, it's flattering and it shows that you are not intimidated.

□ *How would you define your profession?*

With questions that solicit your understanding of a topic, no matter how good your answer, you can expect to be interrupted in mid-reply with 'That has nothing to do with it,' or, 'Whoever put that idea into your head?' While your response is a judgement call, 999 times out of a thousand these comments are not meant to be taken as serious criticisms. Rather, they are tests to see how well you would be able to defend your position in a no-holds-barred conversation with the chairman of the board who says exactly what he or she thinks at all times. So go ahead and defend yourself, without taking or showing offence.

Your first response will be to gain time and get the interviewer talking. 'Why do you say that?' you ask, answering a question with a question. And turning the tables on your aggressor displays your poise, calm and analytical skills better than any other response.

☐ *Why should I hire an outsider when I could fill the job with someone inside the company?*

The question isn't as stupid as it sounds. Obviously, the interviewer has examined existing employees with an eye towards their promotion or re-assignment. Just as obviously, the job cannot be filled from within the company. If it could be, it would be, and for two very good reasons: it is cheaper for the company to promote from within, and it is good for employee morale.

Hiding behind this intimidating question is actually a pleasant invitation: 'Tell me why I should hire you.' Your answer follows two steps. The first is a simple recitation of your skills and personality profile strengths, tailored to the specific require-ments of the job.

For the second step, realise first that whenever a manager is filling a position, he or she is looking not only for someone who can do the job, but also for someone who can benefit the department in a larger sense. No department is as good as it could be – each has weaknesses that need strengthening. So in the second part of your answer, include a question of your own: 'Those are my general attributes. However, if no one is promotable from inside the company, that means you want to add strength to your team in a special way. In what ways do you hope the final candidate will be able to benefit your department?' The answer to this is your cue to sell your applicable qualities.

☐ *Have you ever had any financial difficulties?*

The potential employer wants to know whether you can control not only your own finances, but finances in general. If you are in the insurance field, for example – claims, accounting, supervision, management – you can expect to hear this one. The question, though, is not restricted to insurance. Anyone, especially the person who handles money in day-to-day business, is fair game.

The interviewer does not want to hear sob-stories. If you have had financial problems, concentrate on the information that will damage your candidacy least and enhance it most. You might find it appropriate to bring the matter up yourself. If you choose to wait until the interviewer brings it up, you might say, 'I should tell you that some years ago, for reasons beyond my control, I was forced into personal bankruptcy. That has been behind me for some time. Today, I have a sound credit rating and no debts. Bankruptcy is not something I'm proud of, but I did learn from the experience, and I feel it has made me a more proficient accounts supervisor.' The answer concentrates on today, not past history.

☐ *How do you handle rejection?*

This question is common if you are applying for a job in sales, including face-to-face sales, telemarketing, public relations and customer service. If you are after a job in one of these areas and you really don't like the heavy doses of rejection that are any salesperson's lot, consider a new field. The anguish you will experience will not lead to a successful career or a happy life.

With that in mind, let's look behind the question. The interviewer simply wants to know whether you take rejection as rejection of yourself or whether you simply accept it as a temporary rejection of a service or product. Here is a sample answer that you can tailor to your particular needs and background: 'I accept rejection as an integral part of the sales process. If everyone said yes to a product, there would be no need for the sales function. As it is, I see every rejection as bringing me closer to the customer who will say yes.' Then, if you are encouraged to go on: 'I regard rejection as simply a fact of life, that the customer has no need for the product today. I can go on to my next call with the conviction that I am a little closer to my next sale.'

☐ *Why were you out of work for so long?*

You must have a sound explanation for any and all gaps in your employment history. If not, you are unlikely to receive a job offer. Emphasise that you were not just looking for another pay cheque – you were looking for a company to settle with and make a long-term contribution to.

'I made a decision that I enjoy my work too much just to accept another pay cheque. So I determined that the next job I took would be one where I could settle down and do my best to make a solid contribution. From everything I have heard about this company, you are a group that expects people to pull their weight, because you've got a real job to do. I like that, and I would like to be part of the team. What have I got to do to get the job?'

You answer the question, compliment the interviewer and

shift the emphasis from you being unemployed to how you can get the job offer.

□ *Why have you changed jobs so frequently?*

If you have jumped around, blame it on youth (even the interviewer was young once). Now you realise what a mistake your job-hopping was, and with your added domestic responsibilities you are now much more settled. Or you may wish to impress on the interviewer that your job-hopping was never as a result of poor performance, and that you grew professionally as a result of each job change.

You could reply: 'My first job involved a long journey to and from the office. I soon realised that, but I knew it would give me good experience in a very competitive field. Subsequently, I found a job much closer to home where the journey was only an hour each way. I was very happy at my second job. However, I had an opportunity to broaden my experience with a new company that was starting up. With the wisdom of hindsight, I realise that was a mistake; it took me six months to realise I couldn't make a contribution there. I've been with my current company a reasonable length of time. So I have broad experience in different environments. I didn't just job-hop; I have been following a path to gain broad experience. So you see, I have more experience than the average person of my years, and a desire to settle down and make it pay off for me and my employer.'

Or you can say: 'Now I want to settle down and make all my diverse background pay off in my contribution to my new employer. I have a strong desire to contribute and am looking for an employer that will keep me challenged. I think this might be the company to do that. Am I right?'

□ *Tell me about a time when you put your foot in it.*

Answer this question with caution. The interviewer is examining your ability and willingness to interact pleasantly with others. The question is tricky because it asks you to show yourself in a poor light. Your answer will downplay the negative impact of your action and will end with positive information about your candidacy. The best thing to do is to start with an example outside the workplace, and show how the experience improved your performance at work.

'About five years ago, I let the cat out of the bag about a surprise birthday party for a friend, a terrific *faux pas*. It was a mortifying experience, and I promised myself not to let anything like that happen again.' Then, after this fairly innocuous statement, you can talk about communications in the workplace. 'As far as work is concerned, I always regard employer/employee communications on any matter as confidential unless expressly stated otherwise. So, putting my foot in it doesn't happen to me at work.'

□ *Why do you want to leave your current job?* or, *Why did you leave your last job?*

This is a common trick question. You should have an acceptable reason for leaving every job you have held but, if you don't, pick one of the six acceptable reasons from the employment industry formula, the acronym for which is CLAMPS:

- *C is for challenge.* You weren't able to grow professionally in that position.
- *L is for location.* The journey was unreasonably long.
- *A is for advancement.* There was nowhere for you to go. You had the talent, but there were too many people ahead of you.
- *M is for money.* You were underpaid for your skills and contribution.
- *P is for pride or prestige.* You wanted to be with a better company.
- *S is for security.* The company was not stable.

For example: 'My last company was a family-owned affair. I had gone as far as I was able. It just seemed time for me to join a more prestigious company and accept greater challenges.'

□ *What interests you least about this job?*

This question is potentially explosive, but easily defused. Regardless of your occupation, there is at least one repetitive, mindless duty that everyone groans about and that goes with the territory. Use that as your example in a statement of this nature: 'Filing is probably the least demanding part of the job. However, it is important to the overall success of my department, so I try to do it with a smile.' This shows that you understand that it is necessary to take the rough with the smooth in any job.

□ *What was there about your last company that you didn't particularly like or agree with?*

You are being checked out as a potential fly in the ointment. If you *have* to answer, it might be the way the company policies and/

116

or directives were sometimes consciously misunderstood by some employees who disregard the bottom line – the profitability of the corporation.

Or: 'You know how it is sometimes with a big company. People lose awareness of the cost of things. There never seemed to be much concern about economy or efficiency. Everyone wanted his or her year-end bonus, but only worried about it in December. The rest of the year, nobody gave a hoot. I think that's the kind of thing we should be aware of most every day, don't you agree?'

Or: 'I didn't like the way some people gave lip-service to "the customer comes first", but really didn't go out of their way to keep the customer satisfied. I don't think it was a fault of management, just a general malaise that seemed to affect a lot of people.'

☐ *What do you feel is a satisfactory attendance record?*

There are two answers to this question – one if you are in management, one if you are not. As a manager: 'I believe attendance is a matter of management, motivation and psychology. Letting the employees know you expect their best efforts and won't accept half-baked excuses is one thing. The other is to keep your employees motivated by a congenial work environment and the challenge to stretch themselves. Giving people pride in their work and letting them know you respect them as individuals have a lot to do with it too.'

If you are not in management, the answer is even easier: 'I've never really considered it. I work for a living, I enjoy my job and I'm rarely ill.'

☐ *What is your general impression of your last company*

Always answer positively. Keep your real feelings to yourself, whatever they might be. There is a strong belief among the management fraternity that people who complain about past employers will cause problems for their new ones. Your answer is, 'Very good' or, 'Excellent'. Then smile and wait for the next question.

☐ *What are some of the problems you encounter in doing your job, and what do you do about them?*

Note well the old saying, 'A poor workman blames his tools.' Your awareness that careless mistakes cost the company good money means you are always on the look-out for potential problems. Give an example of a problem you recognised and solved.

For example: 'My job is fairly repetitive, so it's easy to overlook problems. Lots of people do. However, I always look for them; it helps to keep me alert and motivated, so I do a better job. To give you an example, we make computer memory disks. Each one has to be machined by hand and, once completed, the slightest abrasion will turn one into a reject. I have a steady staff and little turnover, and everyone wears cotton gloves to handle the disks. But about six months ago, the reject rate suddenly went through the roof. Is that the kind of problem you mean? Well, the cause was one that could have gone unnoticed for ages. Jill, the section head who inspects all the disks, had lost a lot of weight, her diamond engagement ring slipped around her finger, and it was scratching the disks as she passed them and stacked them to be shipped. Our main client was giving us a big problem over it, so my looking for problems and paying attention to detail really paid off.'

The interviewer was trying to get you to reveal weak points; you avoided the trap.

☐ *What are some of the things you find difficult to do? Why do you feel this way?*

This is a variation on a couple of earlier questions. Remember, anything that goes against the best interests of your employer is difficult to do. If you are pressed for a job function you find difficult, answer in the past tense; that way, you show that you recognise the difficulty, but that you obviously handle it well.

'That's a tough question. There are so many things that are difficult to learn in our business if you want to do the job right. I used to have 40 clients to sell to every month, and I was so busy keeping in touch with all of them, I never got a chance to sell to any of them. So I graded them into three groups. I call on the top 20 per cent with whom I did business every three weeks. The next group were those I sold to occasionally. I call on them once a month, but with a difference – each month, I marked ten of them to spend time with and really get to know. I still have difficulty reaching all 40 of my clients in a month, but my sales have tripled and are still climbing.'

☐ *Jobs have plusses and minuses. What were some of the minuses on your last job?*

A variation on the question, 'What interests you least about this job?' which was handled earlier. Use the same type of answer. For example, 'Like any salesperson, I enjoy selling, not doing the paperwork. But as I cannot expect the customer to get the goods, and me my commission, without following through on this task, I grin and bear it. Besides, if I don't do the paperwork, that holds up other people in the company.'

If you are not in sales, use the sales force as a scapegoat. 'In accounts receivable, it's my job to get the money in to provide the payroll and good things like that. Half the time, the goods are despatched before I get the paperwork because sales says, "It's a rush order." That's a real minus to me. It was so bad at my last company, we tried a new approach. We had a meeting with sales and explained our problem. The result was that incremental commissions were based on cash in, not on invoice date. They understood the problem, and things are much better now.'

☐ *What kind of people do you like to work with?*

This is the easy part of a tricky three-part question. Obviously, you like to work with people who have pride, honesty, integrity and dedication to their work. Now . . .

☐ *What kind of people do you find it difficult to work with?*

The second part of the same question. You could say: 'People who don't follow procedures, or slackers – the occasional rotten apples who don't really care about the quality of their work. They're long on complaints, but short on solutions.' Which brings us to the third part of the question . . .

☐ *How have you worked successfully with this difficult type of person?*

This is the most difficult part to answer. You might reply: 'I stick to my guns, keep enthusiastic and hope some of it will rub off. I had a big problem with one fellow – all he did was complain and always in my area. Eventually, I told him how I felt. I said if I were a millionaire, I'd have all the answers and wouldn't have to work, but as it was, I wasn't, and had to work for a living. I told George that I really enjoyed his company, but I didn't want to hear it any more. Every time I saw him after that, I presented him with a work problem and asked his advice.'

You can go on that sometimes you've noticed that such people simply lack enthusiasm and confidence, and that energetic and cheerful co-workers can often change that. If the interviewer follows up with an inquiry about what you would do if no amount of effort on your part solved the problem, respond, 'I would maintain cordial relations, but not go out of my way to seek more than a business-like acquaintance. Life is too short to be demotivated by people who always think their cup is half empty.'

□ *How did you get your last job?*

The interviewer is looking for initiative. If you can, show it. At least, show determination.

'I was actually turned down for my last job as having too little experience. I asked the manager to give me a trial before she offered it to anyone else. I went in and asked for a list of companies they'd never sold to, picked up the phone, and in that hour I arranged two appointments. How did I get the job? In a word, determination!'

□ *How would you evaluate me as an interviewer?*

The question is dangerous, maybe more so than the one asking you to criticise your boss. Whatever you do, of course, don't tell the truth if you think the interviewer is an unconscious incompetent. It may be true, but it won't get you a job offer. This is an instance where honesty is not the best policy. It is best to say, 'This is one of the toughest interviews I have ever been through, and I don't relish the prospect of going through another. Yet I do realise what you are trying to achieve.' Then go on to explain that you understand the interviewer wants to know whether you can think on your feet, that there is pressure on the job, and that he or she is trying to simulate some of that real-life pressure in the interview. You may choose to finish the answer with a question of your own: 'How do you think I fit the profile of the person you need?'

□ *I'm not sure you're suitable for the job.*

Don't worry about the tone of the question – the interviewer's 'I'm not sure' really means, 'I'd like to hire you, so here's a wide open opportunity to sell yourself to me.' He or she is probing three areas from your personal profile: your confidence, determination and listening profiles. Remain calm and put the ball straight back into the interviewer's court: 'Why do you say that?' You need both the information and time to think up an appropriate reply, but it is important to show that you are not intimidated. Work out a programme of action for this question; even if the interviewer's point regarding your skills is valid, come back with value keys and alternative compatible skills. You counter with other skills that show your competence and learning ability, and use them to show that you can pick up the new skills quickly. Tie the two together and demonstrate that with your other attributes you can bring many plusses to the job. Finish your answer with a reflexive question that encourages a 'yes' answer.

'I admit my programming skills in that language are a little light. However, all programming languages have similarities, and my experience demonstrates that with a competence in four other languages, getting up to speed with this one will only take a short while. Plus, I can bring a depth of other experience to the job.' Then, after you itemise your experience: 'Wouldn't you agree?'

If the reason for the question is not a lack of technical skills, it must be a question about one of your key profile areas. Perhaps the interviewer will say, 'You haven't convinced me of your determination.' This is an invitation to sell yourself, so tell a story that demonstrates determination.

For example: 'It's interesting you should say that. My present boss *is* convinced of my determination. About a year ago we were having some problems with a union organisation in the plant. Management's problem was our 50 per cent Gujarati monolingual production workforce. Despite the fact that our people had the best working conditions and benefits in the area, they were strongly pro-union. If they were successful, we would be the first unionised division in the company. No one in management spoke the language, so I took a crash course – two hours at home every night for five weeks. I got one of the maintenance crew to help me with my grammar and diction. Then a number of other production workers started saying simple things to me in Gujarati and helping me with the answers. I opened the first meeting with the workforce to discuss the problems, and my greeting in their own language drew an appreciative murmur. We had demonstrated that we cared enough to try to communicate. Our division never did unionise, and my determination to take the extra step paid off and allowed my superiors to negotiate from a position of caring and strength. Wouldn't you agree that shows determination?'

☐ *Wouldn't you feel better off in another firm?*

Relax, things aren't as bad as you might assume. This question is usually asked if you are really doing quite well, or if the job involves a certain amount of stress. A lawyer, for example, might well be expected to face this one. The trick is not to be intimidated. Your first step is to qualify the question. Relax, take a breath, sit back, smile and say, 'You surprise me. Why do you say that?' The interviewer must then talk, giving you precious time to collect your wits and come back with a rebuttal.

Then answer 'no' and explain why. All the interviewer wants to see is how much you know about the company and how determined you are to join its ranks. Your earlier research and knowledge of personal profile keys (determination) will pay off again. Overcome the objection with an example, and show how that will help you to contribute to the company; end with a question of your own. In this instance, the question has a twofold purpose: one, to identify a critical area to sell yourself; and two, to encourage the interviewer to consider an image of you working at the company.

You could reply: 'Not at all. My whole experience has been with small companies. I am good at my job and in time could become a big fish in a little pond. But that is not what want. This corporation is a leader in its business. You have a strong reputation for encouraging skills development in your employees. This is the type of environment I want to work in. Now, coming from a small company, I have done a little bit of everything. That means that no matter what you throw at me, I will learn it quickly. For example, what would be the first project I would be involved with?'

And you end with a question of your own that gets the interviewer focusing on those immediate problems. You can then explain how your background and experience can help.

☐ *What would you say if I told you your presentation this afternoon was lousy?*

'If' is the key here, with the accusation only there for the terminally neurotic. The question is designed to see how you react to criticism, and so tests manageability. No company can afford the thin-skinned today. You will come back and answer the question with a question of your own.

An appropriate response would be: 'First of all, I would ask which aspects of my presentation were lousy. My next step would be to find out where you felt the problem was. If there had been miscommunication, I'd clear it up. If the problem were elsewhere, I would seek your advice and be sure that the problem did not recur.' This would show that when it is a manager's duty to criticise performance, you are an employee who will respond in a businesslike and emotionally mature manner.

The illegal question

Of course, one of the most stressful – and negative – questions is the illegal one, a question that delves into your private life or personal background. Such a question will make you uncomfortable if it is blatant, and could also make you angry.

Your aim, however, is to overcome the discomfort and to avoid anger. You want to get the job offer, and any self-righteousness or defensive reaction on your part will ensure that you *don't* get it. You may feel angry enough to get up and walk out, or say things like, 'These are unfair practices; you'll hear from my solicitor in the morning.' But the result will be that you won't get the offer, and therefore won't have the leverage you need. Remember, no one is saying you can't refuse the job once it's offered to you.

But what is an illegal question? The Sex Discrimination Act and the Race Relations Act forbid employers from discriminating against any person on the basis of sex, age, race or national origin. In Northern Ireland, religious discrimination is also ruled out.

Some questions verge on the discriminatory, such as:

☐ *How old are you?*

Old-age discrimination is still prevalent, but with older people joining the workforce every day and the increasing need for experienced workers, you will hear this question less and less. Answer the question in terms of your experience. For example: 'I'm in my fifties and have more than 25 years of experience in this field.' Then list your skills as they apply to the job.

☐ *Are you married?*

If you are, the company is concerned about the impact your family duties and future plans will have on your tenure there. Your answer could be, 'Yes, I am. Of course, I make a separation between my work life and my family life that allows me to give my all to a job. I have no problem with travel or late hours – those things are part of this line of work. I'm sure my references will confirm this for you.'

☐ *Do you plan to have children?*

This isn't any of the interviewer's business, but he or she wants to know whether you will leave the company early to raise a family. However, unless the question is also asked of male applicants, it could be considered as discriminating against women. The skilful interviewer can usually elicit such information without asking a direct question.

□ *How should I handle an illegal question?*

Employers are forbidden to discriminate against any person on the basis of sex or race. But what is an illegal question? Employment discrimination, illegal and unsavoury as it is, is difficult to pinpoint, and even harder to litigate. Your best bet is to follow your common sense, to go by what is important to you. That gives you a few options:

- *Answer the question.* If you are asked pointed questions about your origins, or your personal life, and you want the job despite the interviewer's (and company's) apparent discriminatory bent, tell the interviewer what he or she wants to hear.
- *Say, 'I don't believe that question is relevant to my ability to do the job.'* If you want the job, this is a good way to signal to the interviewer that you are aware of what he or she is doing.
- *Ask the interviewer to explain the question's relevance to the job.* This gives you time to clarify both your choices and what the interviewer is driving at.

Outright discrimination these days is rare. With discriminatory questions, your response must be positive – that's the only way you're going to get the job offer, and getting a job offer gives you some leverage with other jobs. You don't have to work for a discriminatory company, but you can certainly use the firm to get to something better.

Interviewers may pull all kinds of tricks on you, but you will come through with flying colours once you realise that they're trying to discover something extremely simple – whether or not you can take the heat. After all, those interviewers are only trying to sort out the good corporate warriors from the walking wounded. If you are asked and successfully handle these trick and negatively phrased questions, the interviewer will end up looking at you favourably. Stay calm, give as good as you get and take it all in good part. Remember that no one can intimidate you without your permission.

Chapter 14
Strange Venues

Why are some interviews conducted in strange places? Are meetings in noisy, distracting hotel lobbies designed as a form of torture? What are the real reasons why an interviewer invites you to eat at a fancy restaurant?

For the most part, these tough-on-the-nerves situations come about because the interviewer is a busy person, fitting you into a busy schedule. Take the case of a woman I know. She had heard stories about tough interview situations but never expected to face one herself. It happened at a retail convention, and she had been asked to meet for a final interview by the swimming pool. The interviewer was there, taking a short break between meetings, in his bathing costume. And the first thing the interviewer did was to suggest that my friend slip into something more comfortable.

This scenario may not lie in your future, but the chances are that you will face many tough interview situations in your career. They call for a clear head and a little gamesmanship to put you ahead of the competition. The interviewee at the pool used both. She removed her jacket, folded it over the arm of a chair and seated herself, saying pleasantly, 'That's much better. Where shall we begin?'

It isn't easy to remain calm at times like these. On top of interview nerves, you're worried about being overheard in a public place, or (worse) surprised by the appearance of your current boss. That last item isn't too far-fetched. It actually happened to a reader who was being interviewed in the departure lounge at an airport when her boss walked through the arrivals door. (She had asked for the day off 'to take the dog to the vet'.)

Could she have avoided the situation? Certainly, if she had asked about privacy when the meeting was arranged. This would have reminded the interviewer of the need for discretion. The point is to do all you can in advance to make such a meeting as private as possible. Once that's done, you can ignore the rest of the world and concentrate on the interviewer's questions.

Hotel lobbies and other strange places

Strange interview situations provide other wonderful opportunities to embarrass yourself. You come to a hotel lobby in full corporate battle dress: coat, briefcase, perhaps an umbrella. You sit down to wait for the interviewer. 'Aha,' you think to yourself, opening your briefcase, 'I'll show him my excellent work habits by delving into this computer printout.'

That's not such a good idea. Have you ever tried standing up with your lap covered in business papers, then juggling your briefcase from right hand to left to accommodate the ritual handshake? It's quite difficult. Besides, while sitting in nervous anticipation, pre-interview tension has no way of dissipating. Your mouth will become dry, and your 'Good morning, I'm pleased to meet you' will come out strained.

To avoid such catastrophes in places like hotel lobbies, first remove your coat on arrival. Then, instead of sitting, walk around for a bit while you wait. Even in a small lobby, a few steps back and forth will help you to reduce tension to a manageable level. Keep your briefcase in your left hand at all times; it makes you look purposeful, and you won't trip over it when you meet the interviewer.

If for any reason you must sit down, make a conscious effort to breathe deeply and slowly. This will help to control the adrenalin that makes you feel jumpy.

A strange setting can actually put you on an equal footing with the interviewer. Neither of you is on home ground, so in many cases the interviewer will feel just as awkward as you do. A little gamesmanship can turn the occasion to your advantage.

To gain the upper hand, get to the meeting site early to scout the territory. By knowing your surroundings, you will feel more relaxed. Early arrival also allows you to control the outcome of the meeting in other subtle ways. You will have time to stake out the most private spot in an otherwise public place. Corners are best. They tend to be quieter, and you can choose the seat that puts your back to the wall (in a practical sense, that is). In this position, you have a clear view of your surroundings and will feel more secure. The fear of being overheard will evaporate.

The situation is now somewhat in your favour. You know the locale, and the meeting place is as much yours as the interviewer's. You will have a clear view of your surroundings, and the odds are that you will be more relaxed than the interviewer. When he or she arrives, say, 'I arrived a little early to make sure we had some privacy. I think over here is the best spot.' With this positive demonstration of your organisational abilities, you give yourself a head start over the competition.

The meal meeting

Breakfast, lunch or dinner are the prime choices for interviewers who want to catch the seasoned professional off-guard. In fact, the meal is arguably the toughest of all tough interview situations. The setting offers the interviewer the chance to see you in a non-office (and therefore more natural) setting, to observe your social graces and see you as a whole person. Here, topics that would be impossible to address in the traditional office setting will naturally surface, often with virtually no effort on the part of the interviewer. The slightest slip in front of that wily old sea pirate opposite – thinly disguised in an expensive suit – could scupper your candidacy quickly.

Usually, you will not be invited to a dinner meeting until you have already demonstrated that you are capable of doing the job. It's a good sign, actually: an invitation to a meal means that you are under strong consideration and, by extension, intense scrutiny.

This meeting is often the final hurdle, and could lead directly to the job offer – assuming, of course, that you handle properly the occasional surprises that arise. The interviewer's concern is not whether you can do the job, but whether you have the growth potential that will allow you to fill more senior slots as they become available.

You can still blow it. Being interviewed in front of others is bad enough; eating and drinking in front of them at the same time only makes it worse. If you knock over a glass or dribble spaghetti sauce down your chin, the interviewer will be so busy smirking that he or she won't hear what you have to say.

Table manners

To be sure that the interviewer remains as attentive to the positive points of your candidacy as possible, let's discuss table manners.

Your social graces and general demeanour at table can say as much about you as your answer to a question. For instance, over-ordering food or drink can signal poor self-discipline. At the very least, it will call into question your judgement and maturity. High-handed behaviour towards waiters and other employees could reflect negatively on your ability to get along with subordinates and on your leadership skills. These concerns are amplified when you return food or complain about the service, actions which, at the very least, find fault with the interviewer's choice of restaurant.

By the same token, you will want to observe how your potential employer behaves. After all, you are likely to become an employee, and the interviewer's table manners can tell you a lot about what it will be like on the job.

Alcohol

Soon after being seated, you will be offered a drink – if not by your host, then by the waiter. There are many reasons to avoid alcohol at interview meals. The most important reason is that alcohol fuzzes your mind, and research proves that stress increases the intoxicating effect of alcohol. So, if you order something to drink, try to stick to something non-alcoholic, such as mineral water or simply a glass of tap water. If pressed, order a white-wine spritzer, a sherry or a beer – it depends on the environment and what your host is drinking.

If you do have a drink, never have more than one. If there is a bottle of wine on the table, and the waiter offers you another glass, simply place your hand over the top of the glass. It is a polite way of signifying no.

You may be offered alcohol at the end of the meal. The rule still holds true – turn it down. You need your wits about you even if the interview seems to be drawing to a close. Some interviewers will try to use these moments when your defences are at their lowest to throw in a couple of difficult questions.

Smoking

Smoking is another big problem that is best handled by taking a simple approach. Don't do it unless encouraged. If both of you are smokers, and you are encouraged to smoke, follow a simple rule: never smoke between courses, only at the end of a meal. Most confirmed nicotine addicts, like the rest of the population, hate smoke while they are eating.

Utensils

Keep all your cups and glasses at the top of your place setting and well away from you. Most glasses are knocked over at a cluttered table when one stretches for the condiments or gesticulates to make a point. Of course, your manners will prevent you from reaching rudely for the pepper-pot.

When you are faced with an array of knives, forks and spoons, it is always safe to start at the outside and work your way in as the courses come. Keep your elbows at your sides and don't slouch in the chair. When pausing between mouthfuls (which, if you are promoting yourself properly, should be frequently), rest your knife and fork on the plate.

The time to start eating, of course, is when the interviewer does; the time to stop is when he or she does. At the end of a course or the meal, put your knife and fork together.

Here are some other helpful hints:

- Of course, you should never speak with your mouth full.
- To be on the safe side, eat the same thing, or close to it, as the interviewer. Of course, this rule may make sense in theory, but the fact is that you will probably be asked to order first, so ordering the same thing can become problematic. Solve the problem before you order by complimenting the restaurant during your small talk and then, when the menu arrives, asking, 'What do think you will have today?'
- Do not change your order once it is made, and never send the food back.
- Be polite to your waiters, even when they spill soup in your lap.
- Don't order expensive food. Naturally, in our heart of hearts, we all like to eat well, especially when someone else is paying the bill. But don't be tempted. When all's said and done, you are there to talk and be seen at your best, not to eat.
- Eat what you know. Stay away from awkward, messy, or exotic foods (eg artichokes, long pasta and snails). Ignore finger foods, such as lobster or spare ribs. In fact, you should avoid eating with your fingers altogether, unless you are in a sandwich bar, in which case you should make a point of avoiding items on the menu which are over-stuffed.
- Don't order salad. The dressing can often be messy. If a salad

comes with the meal, request a side dressing. Then, before pouring it on, cut the lettuce up first.

- Don't order anything with bones. Stick to fillets; there are few simple, gracious ways to deal with any type of bone.

Bills and goodbyes

I know an interviewer who hires high-powered salespeople. Her favourite test of composure is to get the waiter, by arrangement, to put the bill on the interviewee's side of the table. She then chats on, waiting for something interesting to happen. If you ever find yourself in a similar situation, never pick up the bill, however long it is left by your plate. When ready, your host will pick it up – that's the simple protocol of the occasion. By the same token, you should never offer to share payment.

When parting company, always thank the host for his or her hospitality and the wonderful meal. Of course, you should be sure to leave on a positive note by asking good-naturedly what you have to do to get the job.

Strange interview situations can arise at any time during the interview cycle, and in any public place. Wherever you are asked to go, keep on your guard. Your table manners, listening skills and overall social graces are being judged. The question on the interviewer's mind is: Can you be trusted to represent the company graciously?

Chapter 15
Welcome to the Real World

Of all the steps a school-leaver will take up the ladder of success over the years, none is more important or more difficult than getting a foot on the first rung. And the interviewing processes designed for recent graduates are particularly rigorous, because management regards the recruitment of entry-level professionals as one of its toughest jobs.

When a company takes on experienced people, there is a track record to evaluate. With school-leavers, there is little or nothing. Often, the only solid things an interviewer has to go on are school reports, GCSE and A level results. That's not much on which to base a hiring decision: exam results don't tell the interviewer whether you will fit in or make a reliable employee. Many recruiters compare the gamble of hiring school-leavers with laying down wines for the future. They know that some will develop into full-bodied, reliable vintages, but that others will be disappointments. So, recruiters have to find different ways to predict potential accurately.

After relying, as best they can, on school performance to evaluate your ability, interviewers concentrate on questions that reveal how willing you are to learn and get the job done, and how manageable you are likely to be on average days and when the going gets rough.

Your goal is to stand out from all the other entry-level candidates as someone altogether different and better. For example, don't be like thousands of others who, in answer to questions about their greatest strength, reply lamely, 'I'm good with people' or, 'I like working with others.' As you know by now, such answers do not separate you from the herd. In fact, they brand you as *average*. To stand out, a school-leaver must recount a past situation that *illustrates* how good he or she is with people, or one that demonstrates an ability to be a team player. Fortunately, the key personality traits discussed throughout the book are just as helpful for getting your foot on the ladder as they are for aiding you in your climb to the top. They will guide you in choosing what aspects of your personality and background you should promote at the interview.

It isn't necessary to have snap answers ready for every question, because you never will. In fact, it is more important for you to pause after a question and collect your thoughts before answering: you must show that you think before you speak. That way, you will demonstrate your analytical abilities, which age feels youth has in short supply.

By the same token, occasionally asking for a question to be repeated is useful to gain time and is quite acceptable, as long as you don't do it with *every* question. And if a question stumps you, as sometimes happens, do not stutter incoherently. It is sometimes best to say simply, 'I don't know.' Or, you might say, 'I'd like to come back to that later,' because the odds are even that the interviewer will forget to ask again; if not, at least you've had some time to come up with an answer.

Knowing *everything* about a certain entry-level position is not necessary, because business feels it can teach you most things. But, as a vice president of Merrill Lynch once said, 'You must bring to the table the ability to speak clearly.' So, knowing what is behind those questions designed especially for school-leavers will give you the time to build informative and understandable answers.

☐ *How did you get your holiday jobs?*

All employers look favourably on applicants who have any work experience, no matter what it is. 'It is far easier to get a fix on someone who has worked while at school,' says Dan O'Brien, head of employment at Grumman Aerospace. 'They manage their time better, are more realistic and more mature. Any work experience gives us much more in common.' So, as you make your answer, add that you learned that business is about making a profit, doing things more efficiently, adhering to procedures and putting in whatever effort it takes to get the job done. In short, treat your holiday jobs, no matter now humble, as any other business experience.

In this particular question, the interviewer is looking ideally for something that shows initiative, creativity and flexibility. Here's an example: 'In my town, summer jobs were hard to come by, but I applied to each local restaurant for a position waiting at tables, phoned the manager at each one to arrange an interview and finally landed a job at one of the most prestigious. I was assigned to the afternoon shift, but with my quick work, accurate billing and ability to keep customers happy, they soon moved me to the evening shift. I worked there for three summers and, by the time I left, I was responsible for the training and management of the night-shift waiters, the allotment of tips, and the evening's final closing and accounting. All in all, my experience showed me the mechanics of a small business and of business in general.'

☐ *Which of the jobs you've held have you liked least?*

The interviewer is trying to trip you up. It is likely that your work experience contained a certain amount of repetition and drudgery, as all early jobs in the business world do. So beware of saying that you hated a particular job 'because it was boring'. Avoid the negative and say something along these lines: 'All of my jobs had their good and bad points, but I've always found that if you want to learn, there's plenty to be picked up every day. Each experience was valuable.' Then describe a seemingly boring job, but show how it taught you valuable lessons or helped you hone different aspects of your personality.

☐ *What are your future vocational plans?*

This is a fancy way of asking, 'Where do you want to be five years from now?' The trap all entry-level professionals make is to say, 'In management', because they think that shows drive and ambition. It has become such a trite answer, though, that it immediately generates a string of questions that most applicants can't answer: What is the definition of management? What is a manager's prime responsibility? A manager in what area? Your safest answer identifies you with the profession into which you are trying to break, and shows you have your feet on the ground. 'My vocational plans are that I want to get ahead. To do that I must be able to channel my energies and expertise into those areas my industry and employer need. In five years or so, I hope to have become a thorough professional with a clear understanding of the company, the industry and where the biggest challenges, and therefore opportunities, lie. By that time, my goals for the future should be sharply defined.' An answer like that will set you far apart from your contemporaries.

☐ *What college did you attend, and why did you choose it?*

The college you attended isn't as important as your reasons for choosing it – the question is trying to examine your reasoning processes. Emphasise that it was your choice, and that you didn't go there as a result of your parents' desires or because generations of your family have always attended the Acme School of Welding. Focus on the practical. 'I went to Coolhurst College – it was a choice based on practicality. I wanted a college that would give me a good education and prepare me for the real world. Coolhurst has a good record for turning out students fully prepared to take on responsibilities in the real world. It is (or isn't) a big college, but/and it has certainly taught me some big lessons about the value of (whatever personality values apply) in the real world of business.'

If the interviewer has a follow-up question about the role your parents played in the selection of your college, be wary – he or she is plumbing your maturity. It is best to reply that the choice of the college was yours, though you did seek the advice of your parents once you had made your decision, and that they supported your decision.

☐ *Are you looking for a permanent or temporary job?*

The interviewer wants reassurance that you are genuinely interested in the position and won't disappear in a few months without notice. Try to go beyond saying simply, yes. Explain why you want the job. You might say, 'Of course, I am looking for a permanent job. I intend to make my career in this field, and I want the opportunity to learn the business, face new challenges, and learn from experienced professionals.'

You will also want to qualify the question with one of your own at the end of your answer: 'Is this a permanent or a temporary position you are trying to fill?' And don't be scared to ask. The occasional unscrupulous employer will hire someone fresh out of college for a short period of time – say, for one particular project – and then lay him or her off.

☐ *How did you pay for college?*

Avoid saying 'Oh, Daddy handled all of that', as it probably won't create quite the impression you'd like. Your parents may well have helped you out, but you should explain, if it's appropriate, that you worked part time and took out loans (as most of us must during college).

☐ *We have tried to hire people from your school/college before, and they never seem to work out. What makes you different?*

Here's a stress question to test your poise and analytical skills. You can shout that, yes, of *course* you are different and can prove it, but so far, all you know is that there was a problem, not what caused the problem. Respond this way: 'First, may I ask you exactly what problems you've had with people from this background?' Once you know what the problem is (if one really exists at all), then you can illustrate how you are different – but only then. Otherwise, you run the risk of your answer being interrupted with, 'Well, that's what everyone else said before I took them on. You haven't shown me that you are any different.'

☐ *I'd be interested to hear about some things you learned at college that could be used on the job.*

While specific job-related courses could form part of your answer, they cannot be all of it. The interviewer wants to hear about 'real-world' skills, so oblige by explaining what the experience of college taught you rather than a specific course. In other words, explain how the experience honed your relevant personality profiles. Both at school and college I tried to pursue those courses that had most practical relevance, such as . . . However, the greatest lessons I learned were the importance of . . .' and then list your personality profile strengths.

☐ *Do you like routine tasks/regular hours?*

A trick question. The interviewer knows from bitter experience that most school-leavers hate routine and are hopeless as employees until they come to an acceptance of such facts of life. Explain that, yes, you appreciate the need for routine, that you expect a fair amount of routine assignments before you are entrusted with the more responsible ones, and that is why you are prepared to accept it as necessary. As far as regular hours go, you could say, 'No, there's no problem there. A company expects to make a profit, so the doors have to be open for business on a regular basis.'

☐ *What have you done that shows initiative and willingness to work?*

Again, tell a story about how you landed or created a job for yourself, or even got involved in some voluntary work. Your answer should show initiative in that you both handled unexpected problems calmly and anticipated others. Your willingness is demonstrated by the ways you overcame obstacles. For example: 'I worked for a summer in a small warehouse. I found out that a large shipment was due in a couple of weeks, and I knew that room had to be made. The inventory system was outdated, and the back of the warehouse was disorganised, so I came in at the weekend, worked out how much room I needed, cleaned up the mess at the back, and catalogued it all on new stock forms. When the shipment arrived, the truck just backed in. There was even room to spare.'

□ *Can you take instructions without feeling upset or hurt?*

This is a manageability question. If you take offence easily or bristle when your mistakes are pointed out, you won't last long with any company. Competition is fierce at the entry level, so take this as another chance to set yourself apart. 'Yes, I can take instructions and, more important, I can take constructive criticism without feeling hurt. Even with the best intent, I will still make mistakes and at times someone will have to put me back on the right track. I know that if I ever expect to rise in the company, I must first prove myself to be manageable.'

□ *Have you ever had difficulties getting along with others?*

This is a combination question, probing willingness and manageability. Are you a team player or are you going to disrupt the department and make the interviewer's life hell? This is a closed-ended question that requires only a yes/no answer, so give one and shut up.

□ *What type of position are you interested in?*

This again is one of those questions that tempts you to say management. Don't. Say you are interested in what you will be offered anyway, which is an entry-level job. 'I am interested in an entry-level position that will enable me to learn this business inside out, and will give me the opportunity to develop when I prove myself.'

□ *What qualifications do you have that will make you successful in this field?*

There is more to answering this question than reeling off your academic qualifications. In addition you will want to stress relevant work experience and illustrate your strong points as they match the key personality traits that apply to the position you seek. It's a simple, wide-open question that says, 'Hey, we're looking for an excuse to hire you. Give us some help.'

□ *Why do you think you would like this type of work?*

This is a deceptively simple question because there is no pat answer. It is usually asked to see whether you really understand what the specific job and profession entails on a day-to-day basis. So, to answer it requires you to have researched the company and job functions as carefully as possible. Preparation for this should include a phone call to another company in the field and asking to speak to someone doing the job you hope to get. Ask what the job is like and what that person does day-to-day. How does the job fit into the department? What contribution does it make to the overall efforts of the company? Why does he or she like this type of work? Armed with this information, you will show that you understand what you are getting into; most school- or college-leavers do not.

☐ *What's your idea of how industry works?*

The interviewer does not want a long dissertation, just the reassurance that you don't think it works along the same lines as a registered charity. Your understanding should be something like this: 'The role of any company is to make as much money as possible, as quickly and efficiently as possible, and in a manner that will encourage repeat business from the existing client base and new business from word of mouth recommendation and reputation.' Finish with the observation that it is every employee's role to play his or her part as a team member in order to achieve these goals.

☐ *What do you know about our company?*

You can't answer this question unless you have enough interest to research the company thoroughly. If you don't, you should expect someone who has made the effort to get the job.

☐ *What do you think determines progress in a good company?*

Your answer will include all the positive personality traits you have been illustrating throughout the interview. Include allusions to the listening profile, determination, ability to take the rough with the smooth, and the good fortune to have a manager who wants you to develop.

☐ *Do you think exam results should be considered by first employers?*

If your results were good, the answer is obviously yes. If they weren't, your answer needs a little more thought. 'Of course, an employer should take everything into consideration, and along with exam passes will be an evaluation of willingness, manageability, an understanding of how business works, and actual work experience. These things combined can be more valuable than results alone.'

137

Many virtuous candidates are called for entry-level interviews, but only those who prepare themselves to answer the tougher questions will be chosen. Interviews for school-leavers are partly sales presentations. And the more you interview, the better you get, so don't leave preparing for them until the last minute. Start now and hone your skills to get a head start on your peers. Finally, here's what a professor from a top notch business school once told me: 'You are taking a new product to market. So, you've got to analyse what it can do, who is likely to be interested, and how you are going to sell it to them.'

Chapter 16

The Graceful Exit

To paraphrase Shakespeare, all the world's a stage and all the people on it merely players making their entrances and exits. Curtains rise and fall, and your powerful performance must be capped with a professional and memorable exit. To ensure you leave the right impression, this chapter will review the do's and don'ts of leaving an interview.

A signal that the interview is drawing to a close comes when you are asked whether you have any final questions. Ask your own questions and, by doing so, highlight your strengths and show your enthusiasm. Your goal at the interview is to generate a job offer, so you should find it easy to avoid the crimes that damage your case.

Don'ts

1. *Do not discuss salary, holidays or benefits.* It is not that the questions are invalid, just that the timing is wrong. Bringing these topics up before you have an offer is asking what the company can do for you; instead, you should be saying what you can do for the company. These topics are part of the negotiation, and without an offer you have nothing to negotiate. See Chapter 19 on negotiating an offer.

2. *Don't press for an early decision.* Interviewees *should* ask: 'When will I know your decision?' On hearing the answer, however, they should *not* ask for a decision to be made earlier. And *don't* try to use 'the-other-opportunities-I-have-to-consider' gambit as leverage. This annoys the interviewer, makes you look foolish and makes you negotiate from a position of weakness. Timing is everything, and how to handle 'other opportunities' as leverage, *correctly*, is explored later in Part 4.

3. *Don't show discouragement.* Sometimes a job offer can occur on the spot. Most times it does not. Don't show discouragement if you are not offered the job at the interview, because it shows a

lack of self-esteem and determination. Avoiding a bad impression is merely the foundation of leaving a good one. The right image to leave is one of enthusiasm, guts and openness – just the traits you have been projecting throughout the interview.

4. *Don't ask for an evaluation of your interview performance.* That forces the issue and puts the interviewer in an awkward position. You *can* say that you want the job, and ask what you have to do to get it.

Do's

1. *Ask appropriate job-related questions.* When the opportunity comes to ask any final questions, review your notes. Bring up any relevant strengths that haven't been addressed.

2. *Show decisiveness.* If you are offered the job, react with enthusiasm. Then sleep on it. If it's possible to do so without making a formal acceptance lock the job up now and put yourself in control; you can always change your mind later. Before you make any commitment, read Chapter 19 on negotiating an offer.

3. *When you are interviewed by more than one person, be sure you have the correct spelling of their names.* 'I enjoyed meeting your colleagues, Ms Smith. Could you give me the correct spelling of their names, please?' This question will give you the names you forgot in the heat of battle, and will demonstrate your consideration.

4. *Review the job's requirements with the interviewer and match them point by point with your skills and attributes.*

5. *Find out if this is the only interview.* If so, you must ask for the job in a positive and enthusiastic manner. Find out the timescale for a decision and finish with: 'I am very enthusiastic about the job and the contributions I can make. If your decision will be made by the 15th, what must I do in the meantime to assure I get the job?'

6. *Ask for the next interview.* When there are subsequent interviews in the hiring procedure, ask for the next interview in the same honest and forthright manner. 'Is now a good time to arrange our next meeting?' If you do not ask, you do not get.

7. *A good leading question to ask is, 'Until I hear from you again, what particular aspects of the job and this interview should I be considering?'*

8. *Always depart in the same polite and assured manner in which you entered.* Look the interviewer in the eyes, put a smile on your face

(there's no need to grin), give a firm handshake, and say, 'This has been an exciting meeting for me. This is a job I can do, and I feel I can contribute to your goals, because the atmosphere here seems conducive to doing my very best work. When do we speak again?'

Part 4
Finishing Touches

The successful completion of the first meeting is a big stride towards getting job offers, but it is not the end of your job hunt.

A company rarely hires the first competent person it sees. In the current climate, a company has a vast field from which to choose. A manager will sometimes interview as many as 15 people for a particular job, but the strain and pace of conducting interviews naturally dim the memory of each applicant. Unless you are the last person to be interviewed, the impression you make will fade with each subsequent interview that the interviewer undertakes. And if you are not remembered, you will not be offered the job. You must develop a strategy to keep your name and skills constantly in the forefront of the interviewer's mind. These finishing touches often make all the difference.

Some of the suggestions here may not seem earth-shattering, but merely a demonstration of your manners, enthusiasm and determination. But remember that today *all* employers are looking for people with that extra little *something*. You can avoid the negative or merely indifferent impression and be certain of creating a positive one by following these guidelines.

Chapter 17

Out of Sight, Out of Mind

The first thing you do on leaving the interview is breathe a sigh of relief. The second is to make sure that 'out of sight, out of mind' will not apply to you. You do this by starting a follow-up procedure immediately after the interview.

Sitting in your car, on the bus or train, do a written recap of the interview while it's still fresh in your mind. Answer these questions:

- Who did you meet? Names and titles.
- What does the job entail?
- What are the first project's biggest challenges?
- Why can you do the job?
- What aspects of the interview went poorly? Why?
- What is the agreed next step?
- What was said during the last few minutes of the interview?

Probably the most difficult – and most important – thing to do is to analyse what aspects of the interview went poorly. A person does not get offered a job based solely on strength. On the contrary, many people get new jobs based on their relative lack of negatives as compared to the other applicants. So, it is *mandatory* that you look for and recognise any negatives in your performance. This is the only way you will have an opportunity to package and overcome those negatives in your follow-up procedure and during subsequent interviews.

The next step is to write the follow-up letter to the interviewer to acknowledge the meeting, and keep you fresh in his or her mind. Writing a follow-up letter also shows that you are both appreciative and organised, and it highlights the urgency of your candidacy at the expense of other candidates. But remember that an artificial follow-up form letter could hurt your candidacy.

1. *Type the letter.* It exhibits greater professionalism. If you don't own a typewriter, a typing service will do it for a nominal fee. If, for any reason, the letter cannot be typed, make sure it is legibly

and neatly written. The letter should make four points clear to the company representative:

- You paid attention to what was being said.
- You understood the importance of the interviewer's comments.
- You are excited about the job, can do it, and want it.
- You can contribute to those first major projects.

2. *Use the right words and phrases in your letter.* Here are some you might want to use:

- *Upon reflection,* or, *Having thought about our meeting...*
- *Recognise* – 'I recognise the importance of...'
- *Listen* – 'Listening to the points you made...'
- *Enthusiasm, enthusiastic* – Let the interviewer catch your enthusiasm. It is very effective, especially as your letter will arrive while other applicants are nervously sweating their way through the interview.
- *Impressed* – Let the interviewer know you were impressed with the people/product/service/facility/market/position, but *do not overdo it.*
- *Challenge* – Show that you feel you would be challenged to do your best work in this environment.
- *Confidence* – There is a job to be done and a challenge to be met. Let the interviewer know you are confident of doing both well.
- *Interest* – If you want the job/next interview, say so. At this stage, the company is buying and you are selling. Ask for the job in a positive and enthusiastic manner.
- *Appreciation* – As a courtesy and mark of professional manners, you must express appreciation for the time the interviewer took out of his or her busy timetable.

3. *Whenever possible and appropriate, mention the names of the people you met at the interview.* Draw attention to one of the topics that was of general interest to the interviewer(s).

4. *Address the follow-up letter to the main interviewer.* Send a copy to personnel with a note of thanks as a courtesy.

5. *Don't gild the lily.* Keep it short – less than one page – and don't make any wild claims that might not withstand close scrutiny.

6. *Send the letter within 24 hours of the interview.* If the decision is going to be made in the next couple of days, hand-deliver the letter. The

follow-up letter will help to set you apart from other applicants and will refresh your image in the mind of the interviewer just when it would normally be starting to dim.

7. *If you do not hear anything after five days, which is quite normal, telephone the company representative.* Reiterate the points made in the letter, saying that you want the job/next interview, and finish your statements with a question: 'Mr Smith, I feel confident about my ability to contribute to your department's efforts and I really want the job. Could you tell me what I have to do to get it?' Then be quiet and wait for the answer.

Of course, you may be told that you are no longer in the running. The next chapter will show you that this is a *great* opportunity to snatch victory from the jaws of defeat.

Chapter 18

Snatching Victory from the Jaws of Defeat

During the interviewing process, there are bound to be interviewers who *erroneously* come to the conclusion that you are not the right person for the job they need to fill. When this happens, you will be turned down. This absurd travesty of justice can occur in different ways:

- At the interview
- In a letter of rejection
- During your follow-up telephone call.

Whenever the turn-down comes, you must be emotionally and intellectually prepared to take advantage of the *opportunity* being offered to you.

When you are turned down for the only opportunity you have going, the rejection can be devastating to your ego. That is why I have stressed throughout the wisdom of having at least a few interviews in train at the same time.

You *will* get turned down. No one can be right for every job. However, the right person for a job doesn't always get it; the best prepared and most determined often does. While you may be responsible in part for the initial rejection, you still have the power to remedy the situation and win the job offer. What you do with the claimed victory is a different matter; you will then be in a seller's market with choice and control of your situation.

To correct this requires only willpower and determination. Almost every job you desire is obtainable once you understand the process from the interviewer's side of the desk. Your initial – and temporary – rejection is attributable to only one of these reasons:

- The interviewer does not feel you can do the job.
- The interviewer feels you lack a successful profile.
- The interviewer did not feel your personality would contribute to the smooth functioning of the department – perhaps

you didn't portray yourself as either a team player or as someone willing to take the extra step.

With belief in yourself, you can still succeed. Repeat to yourself constantly through the interview cycle: 'I will get this job, because no one else can give as much to this company as I can!' Do this and implement the following plan immediately when you hear of rejection, whether in person, by letter or over the telephone.

Step 1. Thank the interviewer for his or her time and consideration. Then ask politely: 'To help my future job search, why wasn't I chosen for the position?' Assure the interviewer that you would appreciate an honest objective analysis. Listen to the reply and do not interrupt regardless of the comments. Use your time constructively and take notes furiously. When the company representative finishes speaking, show that you understood the comments. (Remember, understanding and agreeing are different animals.)

'Thank you, Mr Smith, now I can understand the way you feel. Because I am not a professional interviewer, I'm afraid my interview nerves got in the way. I'm very interested in working for your company (*use an enthusiastic tone*), and am determined to get the job. Let me meet you once again. This time, when I'm not so nervous, I am confident you will see I really do have the skills you require (*then provide an example of a skill you have in the questionable area*). You name the time and the place, and I will be there. What's best for you, Mr Smith?'

End with a question, of course. An enthusiastic request like this is very difficult to refuse and will usually get you another interview. An interview, of course, at which you *must* shine.

Step 2. Check your notes and accept the company representative's concerns. Their validity is irrelevant; the important point is that these negative points represent the problem areas in the interviewer's perception of you. List the negative perceptions and, using the techniques, exercises and value keys discussed throughout the book, develop different ways to overcome or compensate for every negative perception.

Step 3. Re-read Part 3.

Step 4. Practise aloud the statements and responses you will use at the interview. If you can practise with someone who plays the part of the interviewer, so much the better. This will create a real interview atmosphere and be helpful to your success. If there is no one to help you, use a tape recorder to create live answers by putting anticipated questions and objections on tape and responding to them.

Step 5. Study *all* available information on the company.

Step 6. Congratulate yourself continually for getting another interview after initial rejection. This is proof of your self-worth, ability and tenacity. You have nothing to lose and everything to gain, having already risen phoenix-like from the ashes of temporary defeat.

Step 7. During the interview, ask for the job in a positive and enthusiastic manner. Your drive and staying power will impress the interviewer. All you must do to win the job is overcome the perceived negatives, and you have been given the time to prepare. Go for it.

Step 8. Even when all has failed at the subsequent interview, do not leave without a final request for the job. Play your trump card: 'Mr Smith, I respect the fact that you allowed me the opportunity to prove myself here today. I am convinced I am the best person for the job. I want you to give me a trial and I will prove on the job that I am the best appointment you have made this year. Will you give us both the opportunity?'

A reader wrote to me as I was revising *Great Answers* for this new edition. The letter read in part: 'I read the chapter entitled 'Snatching Victory from the Jaws of Defeat' and did everything you said to salvage what appeared to be a losing interview. My efforts did make a very good impression on the interviewer but, as it was finally explained to me, I did not have quite the right qualifications for the job, and finally came in a close second. I really want to work for this growing company, and they say they have another position coming up in six months. What should I do?'

I know of someone in the airline business who wanted a job working on that most prestigious of aircraft, the Concorde. He had been recently laid off and had high hopes for a successful interview. As it happened, he came in second for the Concorde position. He was told that the firm would speak to him again in the near future. So he waited – for eight months. Finally, he realised that waiting for the job would only leave him unemployed. The moral of the story is that you must be brutally objective when you come out second-best and, whatever the interviewer says, you must sometimes assume that you are getting the polite brush-off.

With that in mind, let's see what can be done on the positive side. First of all, send a thank-you note to the interviewer, acknowledging your understanding of the state of affairs and reaffirming your desire to work for the company. Conclude with a polite request to bear you in mind for the future.

Then, keep an eye out for any news item about the company in the press. Whenever you see something, cut it out and mail it to the interviewer with a very brief note that says something like: 'I came across this in *Business World* and thought you might find it interesting. I am still determined to be your next account manager, so please keep me in mind when the next opening occurs.'

You can also call the interviewer once every couple of months, just to check in. Remember, of course, to keep the phone call brief and polite – you simply want to keep your name at the forefront of the interviewer's mind.

And maybe something will come of it. Ultimately, however, your only choice is to move on. There is nothing to be gained from waiting on an interviewer's word. Go out and keep looking, because chances are that you will come up with an even better job. Then, if you still want to work for that company that gave you the brush-off, you will have some leverage.

Most people fail in their endeavours by giving up just before the dawn of success. Follow these directions and you can win the job. You have proved yourself to be a fighter and that is universally admired. The company representative will want you to succeed because you are made of stuff that is rarely seen today. You are a person of guts, drive and endurance – the hallmarks of a winner. Job turn-downs are an opportunity to exercise and build your strengths and, by persisting, you may well add to your growing number of job offers, now and in the future.

Chapter 19
Negotiating the Offer

The crucial period after you have been made a formal offer, and before you accept, is probably the one point in your relationship with an employer when you can say with any accuracy that you have the whip hand. The advantage, for now, is yours. They want you but don't have you; and their wanting something they don't have gives you a negotiating edge. An employer is also more inclined to respect a person who has a clear understanding of his or her worth in the marketplace – they want a businesslike person.

Job offers and negotiations usually begin with talk about money, but that isn't where they should end. You don't have to accept or reject the first offer, whatever it is. In most instances, you can improve on the initial offer in a number of ways.

First, you must find out what you're worth.

Step 1. Before negotiating with any employer, work out your minimum cash requirements for any job. Before getting into serious money discussions, you must know what it is going to take to keep a roof over your head and bread on the table. You need to know that figure, but you don't ever have to discuss it with anyone – knowing it is the foundation for getting both what you need and what you are worth.

Step 2. Get a grip on what your skills are worth in the current market. There are a number of ways to do this. Consider the resources and methods outlined below.

- You may be able to find out the salary range for the level above you and the level beneath you at the company in question.
- Your local Jobcentre may have salary ranges available for inspection.
- Ask headhunters – they know better than anyone what the market will bear. You should, as a matter of career prudence, establish an ongoing relationship with a reputable headhunter, because you never know when his or her services will come in handy.

- Many professional journals publish annual salary surveys that you can consult. Look at the job advertisements in newspapers.
- Contact your trade union or professional association.
- Consult your friends and acquaintances – your 'network' – in your profession or trade and ask them about salary ranges in their companies.

In short, find out the minimum you can live on, and find out the going rate in today's marketplace. The first is for your personal consumption and unlikely ever to be raised in your negotiations. The second is for the negotiation time, so that your real area of discussion is, 'What is this job worth to the employer?'

Negotiate when you can

I have said throughout this book that your sole aim at the interview is to get the job offer, because without it you have nothing to negotiate. Once the offer is extended, the time to negotiate has arrived, and there will never be a more opportune time. Your relationship with the potential employer has gone through a number of distinct changes: from, 'Perhaps we should speak to this one', to, 'Yes, he might be able to do the job', through, 'This is the top candidate; we really like him and want to have him on board.' But now is the only point in the relationship when you will have the upper hand. Enjoy it while you can.

The salary you accept for your next job will affect your earning capabilities for many years to come. A lack of negotiating know-how now that costs, say, £1,000 for a 30-year-old turns into £30,000 by the time he or she reaches retirement – and even more when you consider that every salary review based on the higher negotiated salary would make lifetime earnings that much greater.

Although questions of salary are usually brought up after you are under serious consideration, you must be careful to avoid putting yourself into a corner when you fill out the initial company application form that contains a request for required salary. Usually you can get away with 'open' as a response; sometimes the form will instruct you not to write 'open', in which case you can write 'negotiable', or 'competitive'.

So much for basic considerations. Let's move on to the money questions that are likely to be flying around the room.

The salary/job negotiation begins in earnest in two ways. The interviewer can bring up the topic with statements like

- 'How do you think you would like working here?'
- 'People with your background always fit in well with us.'
- 'You could make a real contribution here.'
- 'Well, you certainly seem to have what it takes.'

Or, if it is clearly appropriate to do so, you can bring on the negotiating stage. In that case, you can make mirror images of the above, which make the interviewer face the fact that you certainly are able to do the job, and that the time has therefore come to talk frankly:

- 'How do you think I would fit in with the group?'
- 'I feel my background and experience would definitely complement the department, don't you?'
- 'I think I could make a real contribution here. What do you think?'
- 'I know I have what it takes to do this job. What questions are lingering in your mind?'

Now then. What do you do when the question of money is brought up before you have enough details about the job to negotiate from a position of knowledge and strength? Postpone money talk until you have the facts in hand. Do that by asking something like: 'I still have one or two questions about my responsibilities, and it will be easier for me to talk about money when I have cleared them up. Could I first ask you a few questions about . . .?'

Then proceed to clarify duties and responsibilities, being careful to relate the relative importance of the position and the individual duties to the success of the department you may join.

The employer is duty-bound to get your services as reasonably as possible, while you have an equal responsibility to do the best you can for yourself. Your goal is not to settle for less than will enable you to be happy on the job – unhappiness at work can taint the rest of your life. It is far easier to negotiate down than it is to negotiate up. The value of the offer you accept depends on your performance throughout the interview and hiring cycle, and especially the finesse you display in the final negotiations. The rest of the chapter is going to address the many questions that might be asked, or that you might ask, to bring matters to a successful conclusion.

☐ *What is an adequate reward for your efforts?*

A glaring manageability question and money probe all in one. The interviewer probably already has a typist on the staff who expects a Nobel prize each time he or she produces a faultless letter. Your answer should be honest and cover all bases. 'My primary satisfaction and reward come from a job well done and completed on time. The occasional good word from my boss is always welcome. Last but not least, I think everyone looks forward to a salary review.'

☐ *What is your salary history?* or, *What was your salary progress on your last job?*

The interviewer is looking for a couple of things here. First, he or she is looking for the frequency, percentage and pound-value of your increases, which in turn tell him or her about your performance and the relative value of the offer that is about to be made. What you want to avoid is tying the potential offer to your salary history – the offer you negotiate should be based solely on the value of the job in hand. That is even more important if you are a woman, because the statistics tell us that women are still paid less than their male counterparts for equal work.

Your answer needs to be specifically vague. Perhaps: 'My salary history has followed a steady upward path, and I have never failed to receive merit increases. I would be glad to give you the specific numbers if needed, but I shall have to sit down and give it some thought with a pencil and paper.' The odds are that the interviewer will not ask you to do that; if he or she does, nod in agreement and say that you'll get right to it when you get home. Don't begin the task until you are requested a second time, which is unlikely.

If for any reason you do get your back against the wall with this one, be sure to include in the specifics of your answer that 'one of the reasons I am leaving my current job is that rises were standard for all levels of employees so that, despite my superior contributions, I got the same percentage rise as the tardy employee. I want to work in an environment where I will be recognised and rewarded for my contributions.' Then end with a question: 'Is this the sort of company where I can expect that?'

☐ *What were you earning in your last job?*

A similar but different question. It could also be phrased, 'What are you earning now?' or, 'What is your current salary?'

While I have said that your current earnings should bear no relation to your starting salary on the new job, it can be difficult to make that statement clear to the interviewer without appearing objectionable. Although the question asks you to be specific, you needn't be too specific. Instead, you should try to draw attention to the fact that the two jobs are different. A short answer might include: 'I am earning £X, although I'm not sure how that will help you in your evaluation of my worth for this job, because the two jobs are somewhat different.'

It is important to understand the 'areas of allowable fudge'. For instance, if you are considerably underpaid, you may want to weight the pound-value of such perks as a private health plan, pay in lieu of holiday, profit-sharing and pension plans, bonuses, stock options and other incentives. For many people, these can add from 20 to 35 per cent to their base salary – you might honestly be able to mention a higher figure than you at first thought possible. Also, if you are due for a rise imminently, you are justified in adding it in.

It isn't common for current previous salaries to be verified by employers, although certain industries check more than others.

Before your 'current salary' disappears through the roof, however, you should remember that the interviewer will see your P45 when you start work, or could make the offer dependent on vertification of salary.

☐ *Have you ever been refused a salary increase?*

This implies that you asked. An example of your justifiable request might parallel the following true story. An accountant in a tyre distributorship made changes to an accounting system that saved £30,000 a year, plus 30 staff hours a week. Six months after the methods were obviously working smoothly, he requested a salary review, was refused, but was told he would receive a year-end bonus. He did: £50. If you can tell a story like that, by all means tell how you were turned down for a rise. If not, it is best to play safe and explain that your work and salary history showed a steady and marked continual improvement over the years.

☐ *How much do you need to support your family?*

This question is sometimes asked of people who will be working in a sales job, where remuneration is based on a draw against forthcoming commissions. If that describes your income patterns, be sure you have a firm grip on your basic needs.

For salaried positions, this question is of doubtful relevance. It implies that the employer will try to get you at a subsistence salary, which is not why you are there. In this instance, give a range from your desired high-end salary down to your desired mid-point salary.

☐ *How much will it take to get you? How much are you looking for? What are your salary expectations? What are your salary requirements?*

You are being asked to name a figure here. Give the wrong answer and you could be eliminated. It is always a temptation to ask for the moon, knowing you can come down later, but there are better approaches. It is wise to confirm your understanding of the job and its importance before you start throwing numbers around, because you will have to live with the consequences. You need the best possible offer without pricing yourself out of the market, so it's time to lead with one of the following responses.

'Well, let's see if I understand the responsibilities fully . . .' You then proceed to itemise exactly what you will be doing on a daily basis and the parameters of your responsibilities and authority. Once that is done you will seek agreement: 'Is this the job as you see it or have I missed anything?' Remember to describe the job in its most flattering and challenging light, paying special attention to the way you see it fitting into the overall picture and contributing to the success of department, work group and company. You can then finish your response with a question of your own: 'What figure did you have in mind for someone with my track record?' or, 'What range has been authorised for this position?' Your answer will include, in part, something along the lines of, 'I believe my skills and experience will warrant a starting salary between _____ and _____.'

You also could ask, 'What would be the salary range for someone with my experience and skills?' or, 'I naturally want to make as much as my background and skills will allow. If I am right for the job, and I think my credentials demonstrate that I am, I am sure you will make me a fair offer. What figure do you have in mind?'

Another good response is: 'I would expect a salary appropriate to my experience and ability to do the job successfully. What range do you have in mind?'

Such questions will get the interviewer to reveal the salary range, and concentrate his or her attention on the challenges of the job and your ability to accept and work with those challenges.

When you are given a range, you can adjust your money requirements appropriately, latching on to the upper part of the range. For example, if the range is £30,000–£35,000 a year, you can come back with a range of £34,000–£37,000.

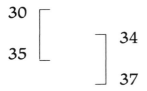

Consequently, your response will include: 'That certainly means we have something to talk about. While your range is £30,000–£35,000, I am looking for a minimum of £34,000 with an ideal of £37,000. Tell me, what flexibility is there at the top of your salary range?' You need to know to put yourself in the strongest negotiating position, and this is the perfect time and opportunity to gain the information and the advantage.

All this fencing is aimed at getting the interviewer to show his or her hand first. Ask for too much, and it's 'Oh dear, I'm afraid you're over-qualified – to which you can reply, 'So overpay me.' (Actually, that works when you can carry it off with an ingratiating smile.) If your request is too low, you are likely to be ruled out as lacking the appropriate experience.

When you have tried to get the interviewer to name a range and failed, you must come up with specific pounds and pence. At this point, the key is to understand that all jobs have salary ranges attached to them. Consequently, the last thing you will ever do is come back with a specific pound figure – that traps you. Instead, you will mention your own range, which will not be from your minimum to your maximum but rather from your midpoint to your maximum. Remember, you can always negotiate down, but can rarely negotiate up.

☐ *What kind of salary are you worth?*

This is a how-much-do-you-want question with a slight twist. It is asking you to name a desired figure, but the twist is that it also asks you to justify that figure. It requires that you demonstrate careful analysis of your worth, industry norms and job requirements. You are recommended to try for a higher figure rather than a lower one. 'Having compared my background and experience with industry norms and salary surveys, I feel my general worth is in the region of £X to £Y. My general background and credentials fit your needs, and my first-hand knowledge of the specific challenges and projects I would face in this job are an exact match, so I feel worthy of justifying an offer towards the top of this range. Don't you agree?'

After your response to a salary question, you can expect to hear, 'That's too much', or, 'Oh, that is more than we were hoping to pay', or, 'That would be stretching the budget to breaking point.' When that happens, accept it as no more than a negotiating gambit and come back with your own calm rebuttal: 'What did you have in mind?'

□ *What do you hope to be earning two to five years from now?*

A difficult question. The interviewer is probing your desired career and earning path and is trying to see whether you have your sights set high enough – or too high. Perhaps a jocular tone won't hurt here: 'I'd like to be earning just about as much as my boss!' Then, throw the ball back with your own question: 'How much is it possible to make here?'

If you give a specific figure, the interviewer is going to want justification. If you come up with a salary range, you are advised also to have a justified career path to go along with it.

You could also say, 'In two years, I will have finished my IPM qualifications, so with that plus my additional experience, industry norms say I should be earning between £X and £Y. I would hope to be earning at least within that range, but I hope that, with a proven track record of contributions, I would be making above the norm.' The trick is to use industry statistics as the backbone of your argument, express confidence in doing better than the norm, and whenever possible stay away from specific job titles unless pressed.

□ *Do you think people in your occupation should be paid more?*

This one can be used before serious salary negotiation to probe your awareness of how your job really contributes to the bottom line. Or it can occur in the middle of salary negotiations to throw you off balance. The safe and correct answer is to straddle the fence. 'Most jobs have salary ranges that reflect the job's relative importance and contribution to a company. And those salary ranges reflect the norm for the great majority of people within that profession. That does not mean, however, that the extraordinary people in such a group are not recognised for their extra performance and skills. There are always exceptions to the rule.'

Good offers, poor offers

After a period of bantering back and forth like this, the interviewer names a figure – meant as a legitimate offer, it is to be hoped. If you aren't sure, qualify it: 'Let me see if I understand you correctly. Are you formally offering me the position at £X a year?'

The formal offer can fall into one of two categories:

- *It sounds fair and equitable.* In that case, you still want to negotiate for a little more – employers almost expect it of you, so don't disappoint them. Mention a salary range again, the low end of which comes a little below their offer and the high end somewhat above it. You can say, 'Well, it certainly seems that we are close. I was hoping for something more in the range of £X to £Y. How much room do we have for negotiation here?'

  No one will withdraw an offer because you say you feel that you are worth more. After all, the interviewer thinks you are the best person for the job, and has extended a formal offer, and the last thing he or she needs now is to start from square one again. The employer has a vested interest in bringing the negotiation to a satisfactory conclusion. At worst, the interviewer can stick to the original offer.

- *It isn't quite what you expected.* Even if the offer isn't what you thought it would be, you still have options other than accepting or rejecting the offer as it stands. But your strategy for now is to run the money topic as far as you can in a calm and businesslike way; then once you have gone that far, you can back off and examine the other potential benefits of the job. That way you will leave yourself with an opening, if you need it, to discuss the money topic once more at the close of negotiations.

If you feel the salary could do with a boost, say so. 'I like the job, and I know I have what it takes to be successful in it. I would also be prepared to give you a start date of (eg) 1 March to show my sincerity. But quite honestly, I couldn't justify it with your initial salary offer. I just hope that we have some room for negotiation here.'

Or you can say, 'I could start on 1 March, and I do feel I could make a contribution here and become an integral part of the team. The only thing standing in the way is my inability to make ends meet based on your initial offer. I am sincerely interested in the opportunity and flattered by your interest in me. If we could just solve this money problem, I'm sure we could come to terms. What do you think can be done about it?'

The interviewer will probably come back with a question asking how much you want. 'What is the minimum you would be prepared to work for?' he or she might ask. Respond with your range again – with your minimum really your midpoint – and the interviewer may well then come back with a higher offer and ask for your concurrence. This is the time to be non-committal but encouraged, and to move on to the benefits included with the position: 'Well, yes, that is a little better. Perhaps we should talk about the benefits.'

Alternatively, the interviewer may come back with another question: 'That's beyond our salary range for this job title. How far can you reduce your salary needs to fit our range?'

That question shows good faith and a desire to close the deal, but don't give in too easily – the interviewer is never going to want you as much as he or she does now. Your first response might be: 'I appreciate that, but if it is the job title and its accompanying range that is causing the problem, couldn't we upgrade the title, thereby putting me near the bottom of the next range?' Try it – it often works. If it doesn't, it is probably time to move to other negotiable aspects of the job offer.

But not before one last try. You can take that final stab by asking, 'Is that the best you can do?' With this question, you must look the interviewer directly in the eye, ask the question and maintain eye contact. It works surprisingly well. You should also remember to try it as a closing gambit *at the very end of negotiations* when you have received everything you can hope for. You may get a surprise.

Negotiating your future salary

At this point, you have probably discussed present salary as much as you reasonably can (for a while, anyway), so the time has come to shift the conversation to future remuneration.

'Even though the offer isn't quite what I'd hoped for to start the job, I am still interested. Can we talk about the future for a while?' Then you move the conversation to an on-the-job focus. Here are a few arrangements corporate headhunters frequently negotiate for their recruits.

- *A single, lump-sum signing bonus*. Nice to have, though it is money here today and gone tomorrow. Don't make the mistake of adding it on to the base salary. If you get a £2,500 signing bonus, that money won't be included in your year-end review – your rise will be based on your actual salary, so the bonus is a little less meaningful than it appears.

- *A 60-, 90- or 120-day performance review with rise attached.* You can frequently negotiate a minimum percentage increase here, if you have confidence in your abilities.
- *A title promotion and rise* after two, three or four months.
- *A bonus.* When you hear talk about a year-end bonus, don't rely on 'what it's going to be this year' or 'what it was last year' because the actual bonus will never bear any resemblance to either figure. Base the realism of any bonus expectations on a five-year performance history.
- *Things other than cash.* Also in the realm of real disposable income are things like a company car, petrol, maintenance and insurance. They represent hard cash that you would not have to spend. It's not unusual to hear of employers paying car or insurance allowances, paying servicing bills for your personal car, or paying for petrol up to a certain amount each month. But if you don't ask, you can never expect an employer to offer. What have you got to lose? Remember, though, to get any of those unusual goodies in writing – even respectable managers in respected companies can suffer amnesia.

Questions to evaluate the offer

No two negotiations are going to be alike, so there is no absolute model you can follow. Nevertheless, when you have addressed present and future remuneration, this might be the time to get some more information on the company and the job itself.

Even if you haven't agreed on money, you are probably beginning to get a feeling as to whether or not you can put the deal together; you know the employer wants to. Many of the following questions will be appropriate here; some might even be appropriate at other times during the interview cycle.

Full knowledge of all the relevant facts is critical to your successful final negotiation of money and benefits. Your prudent selection of questions from this list will help you to negotiate the best offers and choose the right job for you. (At this point, asking some pertinent questions from the following list also serves as a decompression device of sorts for both parties.)

The questions come in these categories:

- Nuts-and-bolts job clarification;
- Job and department growth;
- Corporate culture;
- Company growth and direction.

The following section is also worth reading between first and second interviews.

Nuts and bolts job clarification

First, if you have career aspirations, you want to work in an outfit that believes in promoting from within. To find out, ask a few of these questions.

How long has the job been open? Why is it open? Who held the job last? What is he or she doing now? Promoted, fired, left of own accord? How long was he or she in that job? How many people have held this job in the last three years? Where are they now? How often and how many people have been promoted from this position – and to where?

Other questions that might follow would include:

□ *What is the timetable for filling the position?*

The longer the job has been open and the tighter the timescale for filling it, the better your leverage. That can also be determined by asking, 'When do you need me to start? Why on that date particularly?'

□ *What are the first projects to be addressed?* or, *What are the major problems to be tackled and resolved?*

□ *What do you consider the five most important day-to-day responsibilities of this job? Why?*

□ *What personality traits do you consider critical to success in this job?*

□ *How do you see me complementing the existing group?*

□ *Will I be working with a team, or on my own? What will be my responsibilities as a team member? What will be my leadership responsibilities?*

□ *How much overtime is involved?*

□ *How much travel is involved?* and, *How much overnight travel?*

With overnight travel you need to find out the number of days per week and month; and, more important, whether you will be paid for weekend days or given time off in lieu. I have known companies who regularly expect you to get home from a long weekend trip at one o'clock in the morning and be at work at 9.30 on Monday – all without extra pay or time off in lieu.

☐ *How frequent are performance and salary reviews? And what are they based on – standard rises for all, or are they weighted towards merit and performance?*

☐ *How does the performance appraisal and reward system work? Exactly how are outstanding employees recognised, judged and rewarded?*

☐ *What is the complete financial package for someone at my level?*

Job and department growth

Not everyone wants a career path – in fact, careers and career paths are fairly new to business and are a phenomenon of the latter part of the twentieth century. The fast track may or may not be for you. Gauging the potential for professional growth in a job is very important for some; for others, it comes slightly lower down the list. Even if you aren't striving to head the corporation in the next few years, you will still want to know what the promotional and growth expectations are so that you don't end up with a company expecting you to scale the heights.

☐ *To what extent are the functions of the department recognised as important and worthy of review by upper management?*

If upper management takes an interest in the doings of your work group, rest assured you are in a visible position for recognition and reward.

☐ *Where and how does my department fit into the company pecking order?*

☐ *What does the department hope to achieve in the next two to three years? How will that help the company? How will it be recognised by the company?*

☐ *What do you see as the strengths of the department? What do you see as weaknesses that you want to turn into strengths?*

☐ *What role would you hope I would play in these goals?*

☐ *What informal/formal benchmarks will you use to measure my effectiveness and contributions?*

☐ *Based on my effectiveness, how long would you anticipate me holding this position? When my position and responsibilities change, what are the possible titles and responsibilities I might grow into?*

☐ *What is the official corporate policy on internal promotion? How many people in this department have been promoted from their original positions since joining the company?*

☐ *How do you determine when a person is ready for promotion?*

☐ *What training and professional development programmes are available to help me grow professionally?*

☐ *Does the company encourage outside professional development training? Does the company sponsor all or part of any costs?*

☐ *What are my potential career paths within the company?*

☐ *To what jobs have people with my title risen in the company?*

☐ *Who in the company was in this position the shortest length of time? Why? Who has remained in this position the longest? Why?*

Corporate culture

All companies have their own way of doing things – that's corporate culture. Not every corporate culture is for you.

☐ *What is the company's mission? What are the company's goals?*

☐ *What approach does this company take to its marketplace?*

☐ *What is unique about the way this company operates?*

☐ *What is the best thing you know about this company? What is the worst thing you know about this company?*

☐ *How does the reporting structure work? What are the accepted channels of communication and how do they work?*

☐ *What kinds of checks and balances, reports or other work measurement tools are used in the department and company?*

☐ *What do you and the company consider important in my fitting into the corporate culture – the way of doing things around here?*

☐ *Will I be encouraged or discouraged from learning about the company beyond my own department?*

Company growth and direction

For those concerned about career growth, a healthy company is mandatory; for those concerned about stability of employment, the same applies.

☐ *What expansion is planned for this department, division or facility?*

☐ *What markets does the company anticipate developing?*

☐ *Does the company have plans for mergers or acquisitions?*

☐ *Currently, what new endeavours is the company actively pursuing?*

☐ *How do market trends affect company growth and progress? What is being done about them?*

☐ *What production and employee lay-offs and cutbacks have you experienced in the last three years?*

☐ *What production and employee lay-offs and cutbacks do you anticipate? How are they likely to affect this department, division or facility?*

☐ *When was the last corporate reorganisation? How did it affect this department? When will the next corporate reorganisation occur? How will it affect this department?*

☐ *Is this department a profit centre? How does that affect remuneration?*

The package

Take-home pay is the most important part of your package. (You'll probably feel that the only thing wrong with your pay is that it is taxed before you take it home!) That means you must carefully negotiate any possible benefits accruing to the job that have a monetary value but are non-taxable, and/or add to your physical and mental happiness. The list is almost endless, but here is a comprehensive listing of the most common benefits. Although many of these benefits are available to all employees at some companies, you should know that, as a rule of thumb, the higher up the ladder you climb, the more benefits you can expect. Because the corporate world and its concepts of creating a motivated and committed workforce are constantly in flux, you should never assume that a particular benefit will not be available to you.

The basic rule is to ask – if you don't ask, there is no way you will get. A few years ago, it would have been unthinkable that anyone but an executive could expect something as glamorous as health club membership in a benefits package. In the 1990s, however, more companies offer membership as a standard benefit; an increasing number are even building their own facilities. In central London you can easily pay over £1000 for membership of a good club. What's this benefit worth in your area? Phone a club and find out.

Benefits your package may include

- Car;
- Car allowance;
- Car insurance or an allowance;
- Car maintenance and petrol or an allowance;
- Compensation days – for unpaid overtime/business travel time;
- Country club or health club membership;
- Accidental death insurance;
- Special employment contract and/or termination contract;
- Expense account;
- Financial planning help;
- Life insurance;
- Medical insurance – note deductibles and percentage that are employer-paid;
- Mortgage subsidy;
- Pension plan;
- Annual bonus;
- Profit sharing;
- Short- or long-term disability compensation plans;
- Share ownership scheme;
- Annual holiday.

Evaluating the offer

Once the offer has been negotiated to the best of your ability, you need to evaluate it – and that doesn't have to be done on the spot. Some of your requests and questions will take time to be answered, and very often the final parts of negotiation – 'Yes, Mr Jones, we can give you the extra £10,000 and six months' holiday you requested' – will take place over the telephone. Regardless of where the final negotiations are completed, never accept or reject the offer on the spot.

Be positive, say how excited you are about the prospect and that you would like a little time (over-night, a day, two days) to think it over, discuss it with your spouse, consult your tarot cards, whatever. Not only is this delay standard practice, but it will also give you some leverage with other offers, as discussed in the next chapter.

Use the time you gain to speak to your mentors or advisers. But a word of caution: in asking advice from those close to you, be sure the advice is impartial – you need clear-headed objectivity at this time.

Once you have the advice, and not before, weigh it against your own observations – no one knows your needs and aspirations better than you do. While there are many ways of doing that, a simple line down the middle of a sheet of paper, with the reasons to take the job written on one side and the reasons to turn it down on the other, is about as straightforward and objective as you can get.

You will weigh salary, future earnings and career prospects, benefits, journey, lifestyle and stability of the company along with all those intangibles that are summed up in the term 'gut feelings'. Make sure you answer these questions for yourself:

- Do you like the work?
- Can you be trained in a reasonable period of time, thus having a realistic chance of success on the job?
- Are the title and responsibilities likely to provide you with a challenge?
- Is the opportunity for growth in the job compatible with your needs and desires?
- Is the company location, stability and reputation in line with your needs?
- Will you enjoy working in the atmosphere at the company?
- Will you get along with your new manager and immediate colleagues?
- Is the money offer and total compensation package the best you can get?

Notice that money is only one aspect of the evaluation process. There are many other factors to take into account as well. Even a high-paying job can be less advantageous than you think. For instance, you should be careful not to be foxed by the gross figure. It really is important that you get a firm grip on those actual, spendable, after-tax pounds – the ones with which you pay the rent. Always look at an offer in the light of how many more spendable pounds a week it will put in your pocket.

Evaluating the new boss

When all that is done, you must make a final but immensely important decision – whether or not you will be happy with your future manager. Remember, you are going to spend the majority of your waking hours at work, and the new job can only be as good as your relationship with your new boss. If you felt uncomfortable with the person after an interview or two, you need to evaluate carefully the kind of discomfort and unhappiness it could generate over the coming months and years.

You'll want to know about the manager's personal style. Is he or she confrontational, authoritarian, democratic, hands-off? How would reprimands or differing viewpoints be handled? Does he or she share information on a need-to-know basis, the old military-management style of keep-'em-in-the-dark? When a team member makes a significant contribution, who gets the credit as far as senior management is concerned – the person, the manager or the group? You can find out some of that information from the manager; other aspects you'll need to review when you meet colleagues, or from personnel.

Accepting new jobs, resigning from others

Once your decision is made, you should accept the job verbally. Spell out exactly what you are accepting: 'Mr Smith, I'd like to accept the position of engineer at a starting salary of £25,000. I will be able to start work on 1 March. And I understand my package will include life and health insurance, a profit-sharing bonus and a company car.' Then you finish with: 'I will be glad to start on the above date pending a written offer received in time to give my present employer adequate notice of my departure. I'm sure that's acceptable to you.'

Until you have the offer in writing, you have nothing. A verbal offer can be withdrawn – it happens all the time. That's not because the employer suddenly doesn't like you, but because of reasons that affect but bear no real relationship to your candidacy. So avoid the headaches and play it safe.

Once you have the offer in writing, notify your current employer in the same fashion. Handing in your notice is difficult for almost everyone, so you can write a pleasant resignation letter, walk into your boss's office, hand it to him or her, then discuss things calmly and pleasantly once he or she has read it.

You will also want to notify any other companies who have been in negotiation with you that you are no longer on the market, but that you were most impressed with them and would like to keep communications open for the future. (Again, see the next chapter for details on how to handle – and encourage – multiple job offers.)

Chapter 20
Multiple Interviews, Multiple Offers

False optimism and laziness lead many job hunters to be content with only one interview in view at any given time. This severely reduces the odds of landing the best job in town within your chosen timescale. It further guarantees that you will continue to operate in a buyer's market.

The recommended approach is to generate as many interviews as possible in a two- to three-week period. Interviewing skills are learned, and necessarily improve with practice. With the improved skills comes a greater confidence, and those natural interview nerves disperse. Your confidence shows through to potential employers, and you are perceived in a positive light. And because other companies are interested in you, everyone will move more quickly to secure your services. This is especially important if you are unfortunate enough to be unemployed. Being out of work is when you need money the most and is the time when the salary you can command on the open market is substantially reduced. The interview activity you generate will help to offset this.

By generating multiple interviews, you bring the time of the first job offer closer and closer. That one job offer can be quickly exploited to produce a number of others. And with a single job offer, your unemployed status has, to all intents and purposes, passed.

Immediately you can ring every company that interviewed you and explain the situation. 'Mr Johnson, I'm phoning because, while still under consideration by your company, I have received a job offer from one of your competitors. I would hate to make a decision without the chance of speaking to you again. I was very impressed by my meeting with you. Can we get together in the next couple of days?' End, of course, with a question that carries the conversation forward.

If you were in the running at all, your call will usually generate another interview or speed the decision; Mr Johnson does not want to miss out on a suddenly prized commodity. Remember –

it is human nature to want the very things one is about to lose. So you see, your simple offer can be multiplied almost by the number of interviews you have in process at the time.

A single job offer can also be used to generate interviews with new firms. It is as simple as making your usual telephone networking presentation, but ending it differently. You would be very interested in meeting them because of (your knowledge of the company/product/service), but also because you have just received a job offer. Would it be possible to get together in the next couple of days?

Relying on one interview at a time can only lead to prolonged anxiety, disappointment and, possibly, unemployment. This reliance is because of the combination of false optimism, laziness and fear of rejection. These are traits that cannot be tolerated except by confirmed defeatists, for defeat is the inevitable result of these traits. As Heraclitus said, 'Character is destiny.' In the employment business we say, 'The job offer that cannot fail will.'

Self-esteem, on the other hand, is vital to your success, and happiness is found with it. And with it you will awake each day with a vitality previously unknown. Vigour will increase, your enthusiasm will rise, and a desire to achieve will burn within. The more you do today, the better you will feel tomorrow.

Even when you follow this plan to the letter, not every interview will result in an offer. But with many irons in the fire, an occasional firm rejection should not affect your morale. If it does, grow up! This won't be the first or last time you face rejection. Be persistent and, above all, close your mind to all negative and discouraging influences. The success you experience from implementing this plan will increase your store of willpower and determination, penetrate to the core of your being, bring your job hunt to a successful conclusion, and enrich your whole life. Start today.

The key to your success is preparation. Remember, it is necessary to plan and organise in order to succeed. Failing is easy – it requires no effort. That means effort today, not tomorrow, for tomorrow never comes. So start building that well-stocked briefcase today.

Bibliography

Some of the books listed here can be bought inexpensively in a bookshop. Most, however, are expensive, so you will find it cost-effective to go to your local library to use them. Many boroughs have an inter-library lending system, so if the book you want is not available, the librarian can usually get it for you.

As mentioned earlier, do not rely *solely* on reference books. Their size and scope often make them a little out of date, and they aren't all updated or published every year. Ask your librarian for the most recent editions.

Business directories and company information

Britain's Top 2000 Private Companies, Jordan & Sons Ltd, 21 St Thomas Street, Bristol BS1 6JS.

Extel Statistical Services, Extel, 37-45 Paul Street, London EC2A 4PB.

Jordan's Business Reports, Jordan's Business Information Service; address above.

Kelly's Business Directory, annual, Windsor Court, East Grinstead House, East Grinstead, West Sussex RH19 1XB.

Key British Enterprises, annual, Dun & Bradstreet Ltd, Holmers Farm Way, High Wycombe, Bucks HP12 4UL.

Kompass Register, Kompass Publishers Ltd, Windsor Court, East Grinstead House, East Grinstead, West Sussex RH19 1XD.

Principal International Businesses, annual, Dun & Bradstreet; address above.

Sell's Directory of Products and Services, annual, Sell's Publications Ltd, 55 High Street, Epsom, Surrey KT19 8DW.

The Stock Exchange Official Year Book, annual, Macmillan Publishers Ltd, Houndmills, Basingstoke, Hampshire RG21 2XS.

The Times 1000, Times Books Ltd, 77-85 Fulham Palace Road, London W6 8JB.

Who Owns Whom, annual, Dun & Bradstreet; address above.

Employment

British Qualifications, annual, Kogan Page, 120 Pentonville Road, London N1 9JN.

Changing Your Job After 35, 7th edn, 1988, Godfrey Golzen and Philip Plumbley, Kogan Page; address above.

Employment Gazette, Department of Employment; on subscription, monthly, HMSO.

Executive Post, Dudley House, Upper Albion Street, Leeds LS2 8PN.

Getting There: Jobhunting for Women, 2nd edn, 1990, Margaret Wallis, Kogan Page; address above.

Moving Up: A Practical Guide to Career Advancement, 1991, Stan Crabtree, Kogan Page; address above.

Returning to Work: A Practical Guide for Women, 1989, Alec Reed, Kogan Page.

Working Abroad: The Daily Telegraph Guide, 14th edn, 1991, Godfrey Golzen, Kogan Page; address above.

The Kogan Page Careers Series

This series consists of short guides (96-160 pages) to different careers for school- and college-leavers, graduates and anyone wanting to start anew. Each book serves as an introduction to a particular career and to jobs available within that field, including full details of training qualifications and courses. A full list of titles is available from the publishers.

Also available from Kogan Page

How to Get a Better Deal From Your Employer, Martin Edwards

How to Get on in Marketing: A Career Development Guide, ed Norman Hart and Norman Waite

How to Choose a Career (2nd edition), Vivien Donald

How to Get a Job After 45: The Daily Telegraph Guide, Julie Bayley

Job Sharing: A Practical Guide, Pam Walton

The Mid-Career Action Guide, Derek and Fred Kemp

Offbeat Careers: 60 Ways to Avoid Becoming an Accountant, Vivien Donald

Working for Yourself: The Daily Telegraph Guide to Self-Employment (13th edition), Godfrey Golzen

Working for Yourself in the Arts and Crafts (2nd edition), Sarah Hosking

Index to the Questions

174